S0-AAG-746

FLORIDA STATE
UNIVERSITY LIBRARIES

MAY 0 1 2001

TALLAHASSEE, FLORIDA

Vietnam – The Incomplete Transformation

VIETNAM – THE INCOMPLETE TRANSFORMATION

PETER WOLFF

FRANK CASS
LONDON • PORTLAND, OR
Published in association with the
German Development Institute, Berlin

HC
444
.W653
1999

First published in 1999 in Great Britain by
FRANK CASS PUBLISHERS
Newbury House, 900 Eastern Avenue,
London IG2 7HH

and in the United States of America by
FRANK CASS PUBLISHERS
c/o ISBS
5804 N.E. Hassalo Street
Portland, Oregon 97213-3644

Website http://ww.frankcass.com

Copyright © 1999 GDI/Frank Cass

British Library Cataloguing in Publication Data

Wolff, Peter
 Vietnam: the incomplete transformation. – (GDI book series;
 no. 12)
 1. Industries – Vietnam 2. Vietnam – Economic policy
 3. Vietnam – Economic conditions
 I. Title
 338.9'597

   ISBN 0-7146-4931-7 (cloth)
   ISBN 0-7146-4491-9 (paper)

Library of Congress Cataloging-in-Publication Data

Wolff, Peter, 1952–
 Vietnam, the incomplete transformation / Peter Wolff.
  p.   cm. — (GDI book series : 12)
 Includes bibliographical references (p.   ).
 ISBN 0-7146-4931-7 (cloth). — ISBN 0-7146-4491-9 (pbk.)
 1. Industries—Vietnam. 2. Vietnam—Economic conditions.
 3. Vietnam—Economic policy. I. Title. II. Series.
 HC444.W653 1999
 338.9597—dc21   98-48942
                                                                    CIP

*All rights reserved. No part of this publication may be reproduced, stored in or
introduced into a retrieval system or transmitted in any form or by any means, electronic,
mechanical, photocopying, recording or otherwise, without the prior written permission
of the publisher of this book.*

Printed and bound in Great Britain by
Antony Rowe Ltd, Chippenham, Wilts

Contents

Figures in the Text

Abbreviations

ADB	Asian Development Bank
AFTA	ASEAN Free Trade Area
APEC	Asia-Pacific Economic Cooperation
ASEAN	Association of South East Asian Nations
BIDV	Bank for Investment and Development of Vietnam
BMZ	Bundesministerium für wirtschaftliche Zusammenarbeit und Entwicklung (Federal Ministry for Economic Cooperation and Development)
BOT	build-operate-transfer
CMEA	Council for Mutual Economic Assistance
CPV	Communist Party of Vietnam
ESAF	Enhanced Structural Adjustment Facility
FDI	foreign direct investment
GDP	gross domestic product
GNP	gross national product
ICOR	incremental capital output ratio
IDA	International Development Association
IFC	International Finance Corporation
IMF	International Monetary Fund
IUCN	International Union for the Conservation of Nature
MOSTE	Ministry of Science, Technology and Environment
MPI	Ministry for Planning and Investment
NIC	newly industrializing country

NGO	non-governmental organization
ODA	official development assistance
OECD	Organization for Economic Cooperation and Development
R&D	research and development
SCCI	State Committee for Cooperation and Investment
SNA	(United Nations) System of National Accounts
UNDP	United Nations Development Program
VCCI	Vietnam Chamber of Commerce and Industry
VICOOPSME	Vietnam Union of Cooperatives and Small and Medium-sized Enterprises
WTO	World Trade Organization
WWF	World Wide Fund for Nature

Summary

In 1986 Vietnam began a process of transformation under the slogan of *doi moi* (renewal), abandoning the planned economy for a 'multi-sectoral economy' guided by market-economy principles, with property predominantly in the hands of the state and cooperatives and with government performing a strong steering function. 'Multisectoral' is a reference to the co-existence of different forms of ownership - state, cooperative, private - with which the explicit recognition of the private sector, previously confined to small family enterprises, as an element of a socialist market economy was essentially associated.

The reform was triggered by the disappointing results produced by a policy of orthodox planned economy after the country's unification in 1975. None of unified Vietnam's economic objectives had been achieved because of gross errors committed during the integration of the South Vietnamese economy and the collectivization of agriculture and because of continued hostilities in the late 1970s and the consequent withdrawal of some foreign aid. Agriculture and industry - with the exception of some enclaves of heavy industry - stagnated; supplies to the people were often less satisfactory than during the war; the country became increasingly dependent on economic aid from the CMEA, which it had joined in 1978, whereafter it completely neglected foreign trade with the Asian region. The Communist Party of Vietnam (CPV), the driving force behind national liberation and industrialization and modernization in the socialist mould since the 1950s, saw its position threatened since, though the war had been won, the struggle to overcome economic backwardness was in danger of being lost.

Transformation began with **some basic regulatory reforms**, which were progressively implemented in the late 1980s:

- the de facto dissolution of the agricultural production cooperatives, combined with long-term safeguards of peasants' land rights and the general abolition of compulsory supplies of foodstuffs to the state and the monitoring of the domestic market;

– the gradual reduction of plan targets to be met by state-owned firms, which were also permitted to dismiss employees;

– the laying of legal foundations for the establishment of private enterprises in addition to the family firms already legalized in the early 1980s;

– the removal of restrictions on foreign direct investment;

– the abandonment of the monobank system for a two-tier financial system comprising a central bank and commercial banks.

Following these decisions of principle a **macroeconomic stabilization program** was implemented from 1989 to 1992 to reduce the hyperinflation to which flourishing parallel markets and the partial liberalization of prices in the 1980s had given rise. The stabilization program was based on a *stabilization-cum-liberalization* concept: a restrictive monetary and fiscal policy was combined with the radical decontrol of hitherto state-administered prices and an adjustment of the exchange rate to the parallel market rate, with a subsequent flexible exchange rate system and liberalization of foreign trade.

The **fiscal policy adjustment** had a particularly drastic impact, reducing the budget deficit significantly to less than 2 % of GDP in 1991 and 1992, which is remarkable primarily because Vietnam received virtually no external economic aid in those years. In this period subsidies to state-owned enterprises were largely abolished, government investment and recurrent expenditure were reduced, government revenue in the form of transfers from state-owned enterprises - and particularly the oil revenue that had recently begun to flow - rose, and inflationary financing by the central bank was stopped. The restrictive financial policy was backed by a reduction in the real wages of the three million or so government employees and the dismissal of some 800,000 employees of the state-owned enterprises.

Although this drastic financial adjustment resulted in the neglect of urgently needed government investment and social services in the education and health sectors, the policy did enable inflation to be curbed and economic growth to be maintained at the relatively high rates of 4.9 % in 1990 and 6.1 % in 1991, thus enabling Vietnam to revert to a growth strategy in the public sector from 1993 and since that time, with GDP growth rates at between 8 and 9.5 %, inflation at about 10 % and a stable exchange rate against the US dollar, to achieve a remarkable macroeconomic performance. As a result of rising propensities to save and invest and higher government revenue, this performance has, moreover, led to a relatively high degree of self-financing for the first time in Vietnam's development.

What caused this high level of stability and growth in the first phase of transformation, in stark contrast with the serious economic decline experienced by other countries in transition?

The first reason was the consistency with which the regulatory and stabilizing measures were implemented from 1988 to 1992. Much of this policy consisted of liberalization measures requiring government withdrawal rather than government intervention. The stabilization policy measures did, however, call for control capacities on the part of the central bank and the finance ministry, which could certainly not have stayed on the restrictive course in this way without the political stability that existed, combined with the ability of the Vietnamese people to survive under adverse conditions. The second group of causal factors is of a structural nature and might also be seen as the basis for the 'East Asian transformation model', which also applies to China and, with qualifications, to Laos and Cambodia:

– As more than three quarters of the population work in agriculture, the liberalization measures and the changed incentive structures immediately led to an increase in rice production, with the result that supplies of this and other foodstuffs to the public rapidly improved and even exports of rice, impossible since the colonial period, were resumed.

- The immediate improvement in food supplies and the rise in agricultural incomes were accompanied by an improvement in the supply of consumer goods, primarily due to the easing of import restrictions and the liberalization of internal trade. In contrast to the downward spiral in other countries in transition, this set in motion mutually reinforcing processes, which had the effect of curbing inflation because of the increase in the range of goods available and, partly because of the rapid growth of exports, enabled demand to develop favourably on the whole, despite the restrictive government policy.

- The state sector in the narrower sense, i.e. the administration and state-owned enterprises, had never reached the same size as in more developed socialist countries. In the mid-1980s it accounted for only 38 % of the national product and 15 % of the labor force. The 'rest' of the economy consisted of agricultural and industrial production cooperatives and peasant and craft family units which, despite all attempts to integrate them into the planned economy, always - at different times and with regional differences - led something of life of their own and had been permitted to operate 'outside the plan' since the early 1980s. The ground was thus prepared for the reform some years before the change of system began, through the growing commercialization of economic relations at micro level and the development of parallel markets for supplying the people and removing bottlenecks in the public sector.

- This flourishing environment enabled the unavoidable decline in production by the state-owned enterprises and the dismissal of public servants to be cushioned relatively well. Employment in agriculture tended to rise further. Small businesses and the service sector formed another cushion, but as the incomes they provided were usually lower than in the public sector, it can certainly be assumed that some public servants suffered social decline. With incomes already very low in all sectors of the Vietnamese economy and with the limited degree of formal social security, the change from one activity to another was not as a rule considered to be so dramatic as in more developed transforming economies. Where the high proportion of agricultural employment, the low proportion of state-owned industrial enterprises and the low level of incomes are concerned, the East Asian transforming economies can also be said to have the 'advantage of economic backwardness' over the highly industrialized Eastern European and Central Asian countries in transition, with their comparatively wide-ranging social security systems.

The economic successes of the first decade of the reform policy in no way mark the end of the transformation process. An analysis of development in selected sectors and areas of activity shows that a great deal still needs to be done to place the process of catching up economically with Vietnam's dynamic Asian neighbors on a sound footing. The doubling of per capita income from initially some US$ 170 in the first decade of the reform is but a first step towards this goal.

During the reform of the financial sector the central bank in particular has improved its working methods by no longer contributing to the inflationary financing of the state sector but using monetary and credit policy control and its supervisory function solely to stabilize and develop the capital markets. Even in the mid-1990s, however, the instruments of monetary and credit policy are still essentially geared to direct control of the money supply - mainly by imposing ceilings on the credit given by the banks - rather than indirect control through refinancing and open market instruments.

Despite numerous institutional improvements and far greater institutional differentiation of the capital markets, it is clear that it will be difficult for confidence in the domestic currency and the banking system to be restored. The mobilization of savings capital by the banks also continues to leave something to be desired, although this is partly due to the strictures imposed by the central bank on the commercial banks in the form of upper and lower limits on interest rates to help ensure stability. As declining inflation has nevertheless permitted a steady reduction of interest rates in nominal and real terms, the cost of finance to the business community is tending to fall.

Credit supply to the business community, especially agriculture and small and medium-sized private enterprises, is slowly improving, but continues to suffer from the burden on the commercial banks of long-standing bad debts of the state-owned enterprises and new burdens arising from speculative real estate transactions and short-term trade financing. In the financial markets the fact that the state has passed the problem of the state-owned enterprises' old debts on to the banks is having an adverse impact. Although this strategy has a stabilizing effect, it also contributes to the immobility of the still rudimentary banking system and so to the underfinancing of agriculture and of trade and industry, which is further exacerbated by the fact that, because of the imperfections of land law in particular, there are not enough opportunities for providing collateral.

The **securities market** has had little chance to develop since government bonds are the only tradable securities available. This is due to the slow conversion of state-owned enterprises into joint stock companies and to the insignificance of large private enterprises. The establishment of a stock exchange, originally planned for the mid-1990s, has therefore been deferred until further notice. Company financing continues to depend on the fragile banking system and corporate resources.

The **reform of the state-owned enterprises** initially consisted of lowering plan targets and giving growing autonomy to management, who nonetheless remain dependent on superior authorities, which perform the functions of owners (central, provincial or municipal government, ministries, the military). In a process of re-registration in the early 1990s roughly half of the 12,000 or so state-owned enterprises were wound up or amalgamated with other state-owned enterprises. The remaining 6,000 have since become financially consolidated and are helping to finance the national budget. The planned privatization of at least some state-owned enterprises has not yet occurred because the party leadership wants to prevent the private sector from acquiring a growing share of economic activity, and both the entities responsible for the state-owned enterprises and the two sides of industry have for the most part no interest in privatization. Furthermore, even the *equitization* experiment, i.e. the conversion of selected state-owned enterprises into corporations, proved to be very time-consuming because of the complex valuation problems involved. Most state-owned enterprises have a positive *cash flow*, having diversified their commercial activities into the trade and service sectors, for example, entered into joint ventures with foreign enterprises and let out plants. Whether this also means profitable capital investment is unclear because the enterprises' accounting lacks transparency.

The greater autonomy of the state-owned enterprises and the lack of transparency as regards title to their assets (who owns the capital they have themselves accumulated?) are leading to processes of quasi-privatization of different kinds, be it through the establishment of private subsidiaries or the private use of the assets, with the line distinguishing the state and public sectors becoming increasingly fluid. By consolidating state-owned enterprises in sectoral holding companies, however, the government has made it clear that it continues to see the state sector as the main pillar of its industrialization policy in the future.

The policy towards **private enterprises**, on the other hand, tends to be restrained. Although the *laisser faire* principle essentially applies, the continuing restrictions on private enterprises in the shape of the licensing obligation and numerous administrative checks and the discrimination they suffer compared to the state-owned enterprises when it comes to access to credit, land and foreign trade licenses are seriously curtailing the growth of the private sector. Few private enterprises, for example, have so far entered into joint ventures with foreign partners. Job creation in labor-intensive, export-oriented production lines, which could be established essentially by private medium-sized firms, is therefore more limited than might be the case if the private sector was actively promoted.

Foreign direct investment is making a growing contribution to economic growth, employment, foreign trade and technology transfer. In terms of projects already completed, it accounted for 8 - 9 % of GDP and about 10 % of exports in 1995/96, although import requirements are still very high, given the limited sources of supply in Vietnam.

Of the US$ 22 billion in direct investment committed by the end of 1996, predominantly by Asian countries, only about 30 % has been effected, mostly with government partners, whose contribution to the equity capital usually consists of the long-term right to the use of a plot of land. After the concentration of investment in the oil and real estate sectors in the first few years since the lowering of external barriers, export-oriented manufacturers of consumer goods in the clothing, footwear and food-processing industries and inward-oriented invest- ment in domestic electronics and vehicle manufacture, for example, are now playing a growing role.

The implementation of agreed investments and the investment climate as a whole are impaired mainly by problems arising in the relationship between enterprises and the authorities. Although the legislation gov- erning economic activity has now been largely completed, the judicial enforcement of claims is still as much in its infancy as the rule of law in administrative action. In their day-to-day business foreign enter- prises are therefore exposed to arbitrary and often unpredictable inter- ference by the authorities, which has meanwhile contributed to a sig- nificant deterioration of the climate and was partly to blame for the first fall in direct investment in 1996.

In view of the locational competition in the Asian region, which is tending to increase with the integration of the ASEAN markets, Viet- nam will have to improve its locational conditions significantly if it intends to attract investment in technology- and know-how-intensive industries that is relevant to its industrial development.

Vietnam has no alternative but to take the principle of **sustainable development** seriously because the degradation of the environment is already well advanced despite the many years of economic stagnation. In relation to population, the country's resource base is far narrower than was the case in other South-East Asian countries when they began their dynamic development process. The main potential threats are the shortage of land and population pressure, advancing deforestation, primarily due to the expansion of agricultural land, and the gradual spread of urban and industrial pollution.

Work on laying the first legal and institutional foundations for the national environment policy began in the early 1990s. If this policy is to be implemented, however, a major increase in institutional capacities will be needed. What is crucial, however, is the realization that, particularly where industrial environmental protection is concerned, preventive measures, and above all the use of eco-efficient technologies that consume little in the way of natural resources, are cheaper in the long run than the subsequent repair of environmental damage. Foreign investors too should therefore adopt *best practice* technologies as defined in the OECD countries' environmental standards for their production processes in Vietnam.

An important criterion for evaluating the success of a transformation process is the **reduction of absolute poverty**. There are few reliable data on the trend until the early 1990s. The first comprehensive poverty profile on the basis of a representative survey shows that 51 % of the Vietnamese population in 1992/93 could be classified as absolutely poor in terms of a minimum basket of goods. Poverty is concentrated in the rural areas, the number of the absolutely poor being lowest in the cities. The extremely low level of consumption by a large proportion of the population, however, contrasts with relatively favorable education and health indicators, areas in which Vietnam rises well above other poor developing countries.

The political consequence of the high incidence of poverty in rural areas is the emphasis placed on rural development. This may result in short-term losses for the urban growth centers, but as rural development must be seen not only from the angle of reducing poverty but also as necessary if migration to the towns and cities is to diminish and as the basis for the development of domestic economic linkages, everything from the long-term economic angle argues for the increased promotion of investment in the rural areas with the aim both of raising agricultural productivity and of tapping non-agricultural sources of income for the rural population.

Foreign development aid did not play a major role in the first phase of the transformation process. Aid from the CMEA ceased in 1990, and cooperation with the multilateral financial institutions and the OECD donor countries did not lead to appreciable disbursements until 1993/94. Since then the *Consultative Group for Vietnam* has pledged some US$ 8.5 billion - two thirds of this having been committed by Japan, the World Bank and the Asian Development Bank - much of which is earmarked for the rehabilitation and expansion of economic and social infrastructure.

As administrative difficulties in Vietnam and complex planning and implementing procedures in the various donor countries permitted the absorption of no more than about US$ 1.8 billion in import credits and project funds by the end of 1996, development aid was unable to play the role in which it had been cast in the Vietnamese government's planning.

Since 1994 the IMF, World Bank and Vietnam have agreed on a structural adjustment program, all the macroeconomic objectives of which have so far been achieved and all the conditions met. In the agreements on structural reforms, on the other hand, there have been various delays, particularly in the reform of the public sector, which eventually led to the suspension of further disbursements of structural adjustment credits in April 1997.

Given the specific political conditions in Vietnam, with its largely un-changed political system, the following **conclusions** can be drawn on the first decade of the transformation process:

–   The 'East Asian transformation model' is non-transferable, since the requirements for its success are not satisfied elsewhere. After taking the long overdue decisions of principle on the introduction of market-economy mechanisms, Vietnam was able to build on mutually reinforcing economic and political processes, which soon produced positive results. A few years of high growth rates, how-ever, must not be taken to mean that the transformation process has been completed. This will come only when the foundations have been laid for economic integration into the South-East Asian region, and especially for the establishment of a predominantly private-sector export industry.

Lowering the barriers to the region and to the world market increases both the pressure on Vietnam to adjust and the opportunities for benefiting from the advantages of integration. The learning processes arising from this openness for Vietnam's strategic groups are likely to result in its economic and social models being more closely attuned to South-East Asian examples, which have adopted very different variants of the 'market economy'. Vietnam must be guided less by a fixed pattern of social development forged in party conference decisions and more by the fundamental factors that form the basis of the Asian economic miracle: heavy investment in human resources, a high propensity to save and invest, macroeconomic stability and flexible accommodation of the private sector. The groundwork for this has been done in the first decade of transformation.

1   Introduction

Most East and South-East Asian countries began to break out of poverty around the middle of the twentieth century. After war and anti-colonial conflicts the economic starting position in Korea, Thailand, China, Indonesia and Vietnam in the 1950s was very similar. All these countries were equally poor; their development prospects were not rated very high since their natural resource endowment was, as a rule, meager.

Forty years later this picture has completely changed. Korea, Malaysia and Thailand are now *middle-income economies*, with a per capita income ten (Thailand) to forty times (Korea) Vietnam's. China too, having begun to integrate into the world economy only in the mid-1970s, has already become one of the largest exporting nations and an economic center of gravity in Asia twenty years later.

Vietnam has missed the boat of this Asian economic miracle.[1] In the late 1980s it was one of the world's poorest countries, with an annual per capita income of about US$ 170. In view of its geographical position and as its resource endowment was comparable to that of other countries in the region, there was, however, no natural reason for its economic backwardness.

It was initially the protracted second Indochina war which prevented Vietnam's economic development and in whose political slipstream other Asian countries were able to lay the foundations for their economic upturn. By the end of this disastrous war for Vietnam, in the mid-1970s, it had the chance of regaining lost ground and consistently pursuing the overriding development goal since the 1950s - industrialization and modernization - at the same pace as the rest of the East Asian region. It was Vietnam's misfortune that, at the time of the unification of its northern and southern parts, the communists still imagined themselves to be on history's road to victory and that the completion of the national independence gained by force of arms was conceivable only in a socialist planned economy. The Vietnamese government therefore saw no alternative but to impose on the south of the country the orthodox model of the planned economy with which North Vietnam itself had hitherto made no more than modest economic progress.

It was not until the latter half of the 1980s that Vietnam began the process of catching up economically which is the subject of this study. The failed unification strategy and the obvious weaknesses of the planned economy system led to a volte-face in the Vietnamese development policy under the slogan of *doi moi* (renewal).

The Communist Party of Vietnam (CPV), which had determined Vietnamese development since the early 1950s, legitimized by its many years of ultimately successful struggle for national liberation, consciously saw the reform policy not as the renunciation of socialism, but as its renewal. With the new concept of a 'market-oriented multisectoral economy guided by the state', drastic economic reforms were initiated without the basic ideological principles - rule by the party, dominance of social ownership, state control of the economy - being infringed.

Not even the collapse of socialism in Eastern Europe and the Soviet Union could induce the CPV to revise its ideology fundamentally. It ascribed the decline in the political systems in those countries not to faults in the system itself but to errors by the political management. The lesson to be learnt from this was that prompt and comprehensive economic reforms and integration into the world economy were needed, but not a reform of the political system.

Given this political starting situation, the parallels with the Chinese reform process are obvious. Without particularly emphasizing this link, Vietnamese policy in many spheres has been guided by the Chinese model, not least with the launching of the policy of reform through decollectivization in agriculture, which laid the political and economic foundations for a gradualistic reform strategy in other sectors of the economy. The Chinese and Vietnamese reform strategy also differs fundamentally from that pursued by the Eastern European countries and the members of the former Soviet Union in that it forgoes the rapid privatization of state-owned enterprises.

This study sets out to describe the first decade of the Vietnamese reforms against the background of these particular features of the East Asian transformation model, to examine some important areas of action for the results achieved and to analyze the continuing need for reform.

The main questions to be answered in this context are the following:[2]

–   How has Vietnam managed to avoid the *transitional recession*, i.e. serious losses of growth in the first phase of transformation, which has evidently been unavoidable in other transforming economies?

–   In what stages and with what results was planned-economy control replaced with market-economy steering instruments of exchange rate, monetary and fiscal policy?

–   How have enterprises reacted to the new environment, and how should the development prospects of state-owned enterprises, small and medium-sized private-sector firms and foreign direct investment be rated? Is a clear strategic orientation of industrial policy discernible?

–   How far has the transformation policy taken account of social and environmental policy aspects? Does the course chosen offer a realistic prospect of poverty alleviation, and is there any chance of the expected development dynamism being geared to the goal of sustainable development?

–   What political and economic interests are involved in the transformation process? How is the new division of labor between the public and private sectors developing, and what prospects does it present for the continuation of the reform process?

–   What role has international development cooperation played during the transition from one system to the other, especially since the time that the socialist partner countries stopped providing aid?

Vietnam's political and economic integration into the South-East Asian region presents it with particular opportunities and problems. The normalization of relations in the foreign policy and foreign trade fields after decades of isolation and accession to the ASEAN alliance are among the essential preconditions for Vietnam's future development. Politically, accession to ASEAN is a clear signal of opposition to Vietnam's dependence on its large neighbor China. Economically, its active integration into a dynamic economic area means both greatly increased pressure to adjust if the planned customs union is actually established and greater opportunities for a process of catching up with the partner countries economically and technologically. As a latecomer, Vietnam no longer has many of the options by which the first- and second-generation newly industrializing countries were able to benefit. On the other hand, Vietnam does have a chance to learn from its neighbors' development and to avoid further costly detours.

The transition to the new system will be completed only when Vietnam has caught up with its dynamic neighbors to such an extent that it can be said to have made up for the omissions of the war and post-war periods. In the first decade of this process, which will be considered in the following, decisive steps have been taken to this end. The ultimate question must be under what conditions Vietnam can complete the transformation process and become - in a further decade or so - another 'tiger economy' in South-East Asia.

2   Failed Unification Policy - Initial Reform Experiments (1975-85)

After Vietnam gained independence from the French colonial regime in 1954 and the country was divided at the Geneva Conference in the same year, the two parts of the country, the Democratic Republic of Vietnam in the north and the Republic of Vietnam in the south, went their separate ways politically and economically.

North Vietnam pursued a strategy of socialist transformation in all sectors of the economy and society that was based on the Soviet and Chinese models. In agriculture it undertook a land reform and compulsory collectivization of the peasants. In the late 1960s, when collectivization had largely been completed, agriculture was typically organized into large production cooperatives, whose members had no assets of their own and were paid on the basis of the amount of work they contributed. Families were permitted to farm up to 5 % of the collective property privately. Many farmers put up passive resistance to collectivization and concentrated their efforts on their family plots, from which they derived a large proportion of their income.

In the industrial sector the few large enterprises were nationalized, and the many small firms were merged into cooperatives. The main aim of the five-year plans introduced from 1961 was the country's rapid industrialization, the emphasis being placed on basic and capital goods industries. With heavy investment in metal-working, mechanical engineering and fertilizer production projects and in the extraction of mineral resources, e.g. the coal reserves at Quang Ninh near the Chinese border, which had been developed by the French, a relatively high level of industrialization was achieved, but the supply of consumer goods to the people and linkages with agriculture remained poor.

In capitalist South Vietnam agriculture was partly small-scale and partly structured as a plantation economy. In the towns small businesses flourished. Large manufacturing enterprises emerged primarily in sectors of light industry (food-processing, textiles). However, political instability and developments in the late 1950s that brought the country to the brink of civil war prevented both the resumption of the exports of agricultural surpluses which the French colonial masters had managed in their day and the economic integration of up-and-coming Saigon with the rural areas.

Despite their diametrically opposed development patterns, the two parts of the country had one thing in common: extreme economic dependence on their respective guardians, the Soviet Union and China on the one hand and the USA on the other. The economies of North and South Vietnam were heavily dependent on imported inputs and, during the war, on food supplies. In South Vietnam imports of consumer goods guaranteed a relatively high standard of living for the urban middle class. The USA's contribution to the national income of the Republic of Vietnam in the 1960s is estimated at over 30 % (excluding military aid) (Beresford 1989, p. 80.). Foreign aid to North Vietnam was similar in scale, although a larger proportion went to industrial investment (Vo Nhan Tri 1990, pp. 38 ff.). In neither part of the country did self-sustaining development processes begin during this period. Agriculture stagnated in the north and in the south. Although the industrial sector had grown, it was almost entirely inward-oriented and very capital-intensive in both parts of the country, partly because of the shortage of labor caused by the war.

Socialist Transformation in South Vietnam

Although the socialist transformation had been economically unsuccessful in North Vietnam, the exuberance of military victory led the government of unified Vietnam to pursue a policy of simply imposing the planned-economy system on the south of the country after 1975. With the greatest possible independence from foreign trade as the goal, the different economic structures - food production and light industry in the south, the production of industrial goods and basic materials in the north - were to complement each other. The target set in the first five-year plan for unified Vietnam was the virtual completion of economic unification by 1980 with the nationalization of large enterprises and trade and the collectivization of agriculture and small business in the south (ibid., p. 3).

Instead, the unification strategy soon proved to be a failure. In the south of the country resistance to the collectivization of agriculture grew. In the late 1960s the once feudal system of land ownership in the Mekong Delta had been largely eliminated when the South Vietnamese government implemented a land reform program and land in the areas 'liberated' by the People's Liberation Army was redistributed. The peasants had an interest in seeing this process consolidated, but not in being collectivized in production cooperatives. The compulsory collectivization was therefore boycotted in many cases; many cooperatives never became fully operational. Combined with the low government purchase prices of rice, this led to a further decline in agricultural production.

The dispossession and expulsion of the ethnic Chinese minority brought trade and small-scale industry to a standstill. Ethnic Chinese businessmen had traditionally dominated much of South Vietnam's economy. They controlled the gold trade, the rice trade and large parts of industry. It took several attempts at confiscating assets and nationalizing domestic trade before the 'comprador bourgeoisie' of the ethnic Chinese Hoa in Saigon-Cholon was eventually deprived of its commercial base in late 1976, with serious adverse effects on domestic and foreign trade and the supply of food to the people.

This was joined by the adverse effects of disproportionately high investment in heavy industry and the simultaneous neglect of the collectivized consumer goods industry and family craft firms. When Chinese economic aid stopped in 1978, to be followed by western aid in 1979 after Vietnamese troops invaded Cambodia,[1] a state of permanent shortages was reached in both parts of the country, forcing the Communist Party to take action.

The Party under Pressure to Reform

In September 1979 - a year after Deng Xiaoping's pioneering reforms in China - the party's central committee decided to permit production and marketing 'outside the plan' in all sectors of the economy. This decision in fact merely put the rubber stamp on a situation that already existed: much of the food supplied to the people - in the north of the country as in the south - came from the small family plots that officially accounted for only 5 % of agricultural land. Many agricultural production cooperatives existed only on paper. In the industrial sector too barter transactions and production by small firms not covered by the plan had increased in response to the shortcomings of the plan system.

It was not until 1981 that the new strategy received the formal backing of government decrees:

−   In agriculture a contract system was introduced, giving the individual farmer in the cooperative the opportunity to farm on his own responsibility and to market any produce in excess of a specified amount. This system was in effect similar to one introduced in China in 1978 with considerable success.

−   In industry the "three-plan system" formally added to allocation and deduction in accordance with the Central Plan (Plan A) the possibility of procuring inputs 'outside the plan' (Plan B) and marketing finished products of any kind 'outside the plan' (Plan C) (De Vylder / Fforde 1988).

Above all else these developments were an ideological breakthrough. The party was forced to admit 'mistakes and errors' in the unification policy and in its development strategy of socialist transformation. The enforced collectivization of peasant farms and small businesses and the nationalization of trade had had disastrous consequences for supplies to the people and had to be revised since reality had long since taken a different course. Family farms and firms were therefore rehabilitated by the party in the early 1980s. Henceforth they were considered part of the socialist economy and no longer, as in previous years, a relic of capitalism (Vo Nhan Tri 1990, p. 131).

The party did not, on the other hand, go so far as to question the production cooperatives themselves or to withdraw the central plan. The members of the cooperatives and the state-owned enterprises had, however, been allowed so much freedom that the commercialization of the economy can justifiably be said to have begun (Fforde and Goldstone 1995, p. 85). This process was also encouraged by the fact that the - now legalized - market prices which had emerged from marketing 'outside the plan' had to some extent become the yardstick for the official prices which continued to be set by the state.[2] The result was officially sanctioned inflation in an otherwise unchanged repressive financial system. The rate of inflation rose to almost 100 % in 1982 and 1983. At the same time, however, production increased appreciably for the first time since unification: food production rose by 20 % from 1979 to 1982, industrial production by 23 % from 1981 to 1983 (Doanh and McCarty 1995, p. 101). After 1983 the increases in agricultural output again became more modest, since production under contract had not lived up to the farmers' expectations. The low purchase prices for the agreed quantities of produce, the tax burden, the disproportionate rise in the prices of inputs and consumer goods and the considerable amount of work that had to be done for the cooperatives led to withdrawal to the small family plots. The party in the south of the country responded with a renewed collectivization campaign, the reason being that one of the principal policy objectives, self-sufficiency in food, had again not been achieved in the mid-1980s. There were repeated cases of famine between harvests in some regions (Vo Nhan Tri 1990, p. 139).

The high rate of inflation resulted in various attempts to overcome the continuing supply bottlenecks by administrative means and at the same time to curb the rise in the prices of manufactures. A currency reform in 1985, which above all devalued the financial assets of the state-owned enterprises, was followed by an increase in subsidies to these enterprises from the national budget even though a 1984 government decree had required them to act autonomously in financial matters.[3] At the same time civil service salaries were adjusted to the rate of inflation, which eventually led to a complete breakdown of public finances and subsequently to hyperinflation of almost 500 % in 1986 (Doanh and McCarty 1995, p. 102). The reforms attempted since 1979 therefore had to be regarded as unsuccessful.

What **conclusions** can be drawn from this period, another lost decade for Vietnam?

– The partial reforms in the early 1980s rightly began with the system of agricultural and industrial production incentives. They were not, however, consistent enough, and above all they were not sustained: decontrolling prices in a generally supply-inelastic economy characterized by shortages is bound to lead to inflation, and in a system that is only partly controlled by central planning inflation can hardly be curbed.

– The attempt to force peasant agriculture into production cooperatives failed. This was becoming apparent in North Vietnam as early as the 1960s and certainly could not be overlooked after unification.[4] It is, moreover, their ability to survive that essentially distinguishes the family farms in East Asian transforming economies, which accounted for more than three quarters of the population, from most Eastern European and Central Asian countries in transit. In the rural areas it was possible in Vietnam, as in China, to build on a viable social fabric in the first phase of transformation, without structures having first to be removed or converted on a large scale.

– The Communist Party did not really initiate the first reform efforts: it yielded to the pressure of a situation that already existed. The supporters and driving force of the changes were the enterprises and peasants who thwarted the party's ideologically influenced strategy by putting up passive resistance or undertaking economic activities outside the plan.

– In South Vietnam the introduction of the planned economy after 1975 largely failed. In agriculture collectivization ultimately proved impossible. In industry at least the nationalized and cooperative firms whose old management was still at hand were able to pick up from experience and re-establish contacts from the not so distant capitalist period once greater freedom of action was permitted. Against this background the south of the country was later able to develop into the powerhouse of reform, not least because of close family ties abroad.[5]

—   The transformation of the Vietnamese economy began in the early 1980s with the increasing commercialization of agriculture and industry. This prepared the ground for the later market-economy reforms. As the state sector in the narrower sense, i.e. excluding the cooperatives, accounted for only 38 % of the national product and 15 % of the labor force even in the mid-1980s[6] and many cooperatives existed only on paper, it cannot seriously be claimed that there was a comprehensive centralist planned economy. For Vietnam it was fortunate that central planning never achieved the intended breadth and efficiency as it did in other transforming countries. Its starting position was thus much the same as China's, but quite different from the Soviet Union's, for example. The peasant families in particular were simply waiting to be freed from the fetters of collectivization.

3   Steps towards the Market Economy (1986-96)

3.1   Regulatory Reforms

The continued rise of the rate of inflation and high budget and balance-of-payments deficits in 1986 had triggered a process of macro-economic destabilization that put pressure on the government to act. The system of repressed inflation, which is typical of planned economies, had got out of control because prices in the markets 'outside the plan' reacted directly to shortages and also had an indirect influence on official pricing. With not only the peasants but also the state-owned enterprises doing a growing proportion of their business in informal markets, the classical system of the planned-economy control and rationing of flows of goods accompanied by price controls had largely ceased to function.[1]

As in 1979, it was again a serious economic crisis that forced the party to make a further corrective adjustment. At the CPV's Sixth Party Congress in December 1986 the new party leadership, which had been installed after the death of Le Duan, for many years the party's orthodox leader, initiated a change of ideological and economic direction. The new development model was to be a *multisectoral economy* in which the government, cooperative and private sectors existed side by side with equal rights. Central planning was called into question; the subsidization of the state-owned enterprises was to cease; the aim was to open the country to foreign trade; the preference given to industrial over agricultural development was to be adjusted.[2]

Following this party congress four fundamental reforms were undertaken:

– In late 1987 family farms were given the right to lease land from the state for long periods. In April 1988 the agricultural production cooperatives were de facto dissolved, in that farmers were permitted to buy inputs and market their products largely as they pleased. With the abolition of compulsory supplies of foodstuffs to the state, the control of domestic trade had also been abandoned.

Farmers' land rights were subsequently further consolidated through the 1992 *constitution* and a 1993 *land law*, both of which ruled out the private ownership of land, but guaranteed the possibility of transferring and bequeathing land on long-term leases (up to 75 years).

– The legal foundations for the establishment of private enterprises in the non-agricultural sectors - in addition to the already legalized family firms - were laid by decree in 1988. At the same time the plan targets for state-owned enterprises were drastically reduced. These enterprises were to take their own decisions on procurement, production and marketing. The dismissal of employees was also permitted. The first steps towards the co-existence of public and private enterprises and the abolition of central planning had thus been taken.

– With the *Foreign Investment Law* of January 1988 the ground was laid for foreign direct investment. It was hoped that the country would be opened up to foreign trade with the abolition of the state monopoly in this sphere.

– In 1988 the monobank system, with the State Bank as the body that implemented the central credit plan, was abandoned for a two-tier financial system comprising a central bank and commercial banks.

Important and pioneering though these political reforms were, they were at first unable to help solve the acute macroeconomic stabilization problems. It was to take another two years of inflation rates of around 300 % - and, no doubt, some changes of perception of the geopolitical situation[3] - before the Vietnamese government established, in early 1989, a liberalization and stabilization program which at last turned the reform begun in 1986 into a consistent package.

3.2   Liberalization and Stabilization

In March 1989 Vietnam began to implement a macroeconomic program which, in its blend of domestic and foreign trade liberalization and monetary and fiscal stabilization, corresponded to the model of an IMF stabilization program in almost textbook fashion. Neither the IMF nor the World Bank was at this time officially involved in Vietnam. There were, however, informal contacts, which were certainly not without influence on the conception of the program. Nonetheless, the measures were designed and implemented by the Vietnamese government itself without external promises of funding and without conditions being imposed.

Price Reform

The first dramatic measure under the program was the decontrol of the prices of almost all goods and services, the exceptions being electricity, petrol, cement, steel and transport operations. This marked the end of the decade in which the dual pricing system prevailed, with prices fixed by the government for primary commodities, foodstuffs and the products of the state-owned enterprises on the one hand and market prices for products 'outside the plan' on the other. The decontrol of the price of rice, the main staple, was regarded as particularly risky, since the supply of rice to government employees as part of their remuneration was at the same time abolished. The immediate consequence of the price reform was a change in the internal *terms of trade* in agriculture's favor: as the prices of manufactures had been raised in several stages in the previous years, while the official food prices regularly lagged behind the rate of inflation, the relative prices of agricultural products now rose.

With the price reform, the structural reforms introduced in the preceding years at last had their intended effect: production and yields increased rapidly, rice yields already rising by 12 % in 1989, making the export of surpluses possible for the first time.

Exchange Rate Adjustment

Keeping pace with the price reform, the exchange rate of the Vietnamese dong was adjusted to the parallel market rate, which was about five times the official rate. After this single real devaluation of the dong, the nominal exchange rate initially followed the parallel market rate within a band of 10 - 20 % (Lipworth and Spittäler 1993, p. 3) and depreciated further in nominal terms against the US dollar by approximately the rate of inflation. From 1992 the official and parallel markets were united. The exchange rate of the dong against the US dollar has since been kept remarkably stable.

Liberalization of Foreign Trade

The exchange rate policy was supplemented by a number of measures to facilitate imports and exports, such as the generous allocation of foreign trade licenses, the reduction of quotas and the improvement of access to foreign exchange, particularly for exporters.

These measures marked the virtual end of central planning and the dual pricing system in foreign trade. Although the trade protocol with the CMEA, with its concessionary import prices for important industrial inputs (e.g. petrol and cotton), remained in force until 1991, exports invoiced in transfer roubles (= US$) were now guided by world market prices, after the drastic devaluation of the dong.

Monetary and Credit Policy

The interest rates on credit and deposits, having been below the rate of inflation for many years, became positive in real terms for the first time in the spring of 1989 (see Table 7). Although this did not result in any significant restriction of borrowing by the state-owned enterprises, the only borrowers apart from the state, it did lead to an increase in savings deposits from 0.8 to 3.8 % of GDP (ibid, p. 16). There was a simultaneous rise in assets held in Vietnamese currency at the expense of gold and physical assets, partly no doubt because of the sudden improvement in the availability of goods.[4]

Table 1:	Rate of inflation, money supply and credit expansion (change compared to the previous year, %)								
	1987	1988	1989	1990	1991	1992	1993	1994	1995
Rate of inflation	231.8	393.8	34.7	67.5	68.1	17.5	5.2	14.4	12.7
Money supply M2	324.6	446.1	233.7	32.4	78.7	33.7	19.0	33.2	22.6
Domestic credit expansion	248.6	395.3	155.1	48.3	41.7	21.3	58.2	40.1	25.1
- non-state sector[a]	344.4	235.5	100.4	21.3	65.5	170.0	177.9	68.0	41.4
- state-owned enterprises	221.9	354.5	111.0	47.2	72.0	36.3	24.7	31.9	17.7
- government (net)	328.0	740.5	288.6	55.1	-1.9	-51.6	102.3	17.6	11.8
a including cooperatives									
Source: IMF (1994), World Bank (1995a)									

In 1989, as Table 1 shows, there was a further sharp increase in the M2 money supply, the sum of currency in circulation and short-term deposits at banks. Despite this, the rate of inflation fell to 34.7 %, a development that was probably due solely to the massive supply-side reaction caused by the liberalization of prices and trade. This supply response can be ascribed not only to higher agricultural production and the availability of imported goods but largely to inventory liquidation. In conjunction with the consistent price reform the legalization of the parallel economy thus had an unexpected restraining effect on the rate of inflation, without massive stabilization measures under the monetary and fiscal policies being necessary. The fiscal situation, with its structurally high budget deficits, had hardly changed at this time (see Table 3).

Figure 1: Rate of inflation (%)

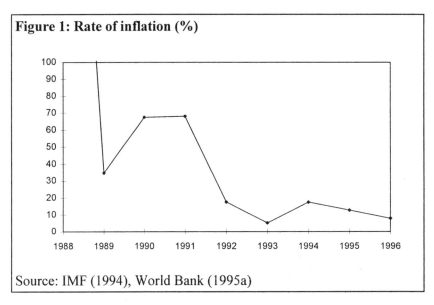

Source: IMF (1994), World Bank (1995a)

The 7.8 % growth of the economy in 1989 despite the drastic liberalization measures confirmed that the right course had been chosen for the reform of the economy. As Table 2 shows, growth was largely due to agriculture in 1989 and to the service sector in 1989/90, while industrial production declined. For many state-owned industrial enterprises liberalized prices combined with the reduction of government subsidies led to the suspension of production.

Businesses organized on cooperative lines also experienced a serious decline, since many of them had been supplied with raw materials and inputs under the central plan and depended on the sale of what were for the most part the products of light industry (textiles, clothing, arts and crafts) in the CMEA markets, which declined sharply after 1989. The decline in manufacturing industry from 1989 was generally deeper than shown in Table 2, since it occurred at the same time as the sharp growth in the construction industry, energy generation and oil production.

Table 2: Growth of gross domestic product by sectors of the economy (%)									
	1987[a]	1988	1989	1990	1991	1992	1993	1994	1995	1996[b]
Real GDP	3.7	5.9	7.8	4.9	6.1	8.6	8.1	8.8	9.5	9.5
Agriculture and forestry	-0.6	3.9	6.9	1.5	2.2	7.2	3.8	3.9	4.6	4.8
Industry and construction[c]	8.8	5.3	-4.0	2.9	9.0	14.0	13.1	14.0	13.9	14.0
Services	5.5	9.2	17.6	10.4	8.3	7.0	10.2	10.9	11.5	12.0

a   Until 1988 the national product was calculated by the 'net material product' system, with the service sector ignored. Since 1989 Vietnam has been guided by the UN System of National Accounts (SNA). The figures are not entirely comparable.

b   estimate

c   including the energy and oil sectors

Sources: General Statistical Office (1995), World Bank (1995a)

Once the direct subsidization[5] of the state-owned enterprises by the government had entirely or very largely ceased, the newly formed government-owned commercial banks came under considerable pressure to finance the state-owned enterprises and cooperatives with credits. As they yielded to this pressure in late 1989, when the structural change for the enterprises became apparent, there was little sign of any hard budgetary constraint on the enterprises. As Table 1 shows, the liberalization measures led to a further sharp rise in the allocation of credit not only to the state-owned enterprises but also to the cooperatives - as part of the non-state sector - and especially to the state. It is not therefore surprising that the rate of inflation again doubled to almost 70 % in 1990 and 1991. The trend in domestic credit creation also reveals, however, that the growth of lending to state-owned enterprises and especially to the state was brought under control from 1990. This was largely due to the extremely restrictive financial policy pursued by the Vietnamese government in the early.1990s.

3.3   Adjustment of the Financial Policy

With a drastic restriction of the financing of the national budget by the State Bank, a fresh attempt to combat inflation began in 1990. These fiscal policy efforts to achieve macroeconomic stabilization were accompanied by structural reforms geared to a change in government's role from centralist allocation to indirect regulation. Above all, this entailed

– the development of a tax system with the aim of widening the tax base, collecting tax from the emerging private sector and ensuring the equal fiscal treatment of state-owned and other enterprises;[6]

– the conversion of planned contributions by the state-owned enterprises to the budget into performance-related taxes and a rate of return on equity for the equity provided by the state;

– the introduction of government bonds as a financing instrument of the state in the capital market as an alternative to deficit financing by the State Bank.

As Table 3 shows, tax revenue from the non-state sector barely rose in relation to GDP after the introduction of the new tax system. The main problem is probably the poor collection of tax from private enterprises, the tax administration not yet being up to this task. Taxes paid by the state-owned enterprises, on the other hand, account for the largest share of total tax revenue now that budget transfers have largely ceased. This is not just a case of exchanging one source for another: about half of the substantial tax payments by state-owned enterprises since 1991 have consisted of levies on the oil sector, which had not previously produced exportable surpluses (IMF 1994, p. 61). The burden on the state-owned enterprises has thus tended to diminish since the introduction of relative managerial and financial autonomy. The major contribution that these enterprises make to the budget is nonetheless remarkable, even by comparison with other transforming economies. On the one hand, it shows that even without a change in property rights the state-owned enterprises were evidently adaptable enough to survive the radical change of environment, the credit granted by the government banks naturally playing an important role. On the other hand, this also explains the government's reluctance to launch rapid privatization, which would have unpredictable fiscal repercussions (see section 5.1).

Together with the significant growth in revenue from the taxation of foreign trade, which can be ascribed to the rise in trade itself and also to the change from import quotas to customs tariffs, there was, overall, an impressive increase in the tax ratio, which within a few years was raised to a level that bears international comparison.[7]

As growth on the revenue side did not begin to have an impact until 1992, whereas CMEA economic aid had been drastically reduced since 1989, the expenditure side of the budget bore the whole adjustment burden. The complete abolition of direct subsidies, the failure to adjust the salaries of public employees, whose remuneration has been entirely monetary since 1989 and so placed a heavier burden on the budget in nominal terms, and a sharp reduction in government investment enabled the budget deficit to be reduced to 1.5 % of GDP in 1991 and 1.7 % in 1992, thus bringing to an end inflationary financing by the State Bank.

Although this extreme compression of government spending on consumption and investment could not be sustained in the ensuing years, 1991 marks a change of trend in financial policy, which was not subsequently reversed: as government consumption expenditure was thereafter consistently below government revenue, the state itself was able to make a contribution to the financing of its investment or - expressed in macroeconomic terms - to the aggregate savings ratio. Besides having advantageous effects on the rate of inflation, which fell to 17.5 % in 1992 and to 5.2 % in 1993, the radical adjustment of the financial policy on the revenue and expenditure sides of the budget thus created a structurally new basis for the financing of the Vietnamese development process: as Table 4 reveals, increased private and government savings soon enabled the aggregate savings ratio to be more than doubled and Vietnam largely to finance itself for the first time.

Table 3: National budget (% of GDP)										
	1986	1987	1988	1989	1990	1991	1992	1993	1994	1995
Revenue	14.0	13.2	11.3	13.9	14.7	13.5	19.0	22.5	24.3	23.9
- Taxes	3.1	2.4	2.9	3.9	4.0	10.5	13.2	17.7	19.4	20.3
• Private enterprises[a]	2.1	1.8	2.1	2.6	2.3	2.2	3.0	3.5	3.3	4.5
• State-owned enterprises	-	-	-	-	-	6.9	8.2	9.3	9.1	8.5
• Foreign trade	1.0	0.6	0.8	1.3	1.7	1.4	2.0	4.3	5.9	6.6
- Transfers from state-owned enter-prises[b]	10.1	9.9	7.2	8.0	8.6	1.2	2.6	1.9	2.0	0.7
- Other	0.8	0.9	1.2	2.0	2.0	1.4	2.5	2.9	3.0	2.9
Expenditure	20.2	18.0	18.5	21.4	20.5	15.0	20.7	27.1	25.9	24.4
- Consumption	13.7	13.7	13.9	15.4	14.7	11.4	14.0	18.8	17.6	17.3
• Personnel	0.9	1.0	1.7	4.6	4.2	2.6	5.4	6.5	8.0	6.5
• Subsidies	3.0	5.3	5.3	0.0	0.0	0.0	n.a.	0.2	0.1	0.1
• Other	9.7	7.4	7.0	10.8	10.5	8.8	n.a.	12.0	9.5	10.7
- Investment	6.3	4.2	4.4	5.8	5.1	2.8	5.8	7.0	6.6	5.7
- Interest	0.2	0.1	0.2	0.2	0.7	0.8	0.9	1.3	1.7	1.3
Deficit	-6.2	-4.8	-7.2	-7.5	-5.8	-1.5	-1.7	-4.6	-1.6	-0.5
Financing										
- Foreign cred-its/grants	2.4	1.5	2.4	1.5	3.0	1.0	2.4	2.7	0.1	-0.6
- State Bank	3.8	3.1	2.9	6.9	2.0	0.9	-2.0	0.0	0.0	0.0
- Government bonds	0.0	0.1	0.1	-0.8	0.8	-0.4	1.3	1.9	1.5	1.2

a   including agriculture

b   until 1990: profit transfers and depreciation, from 1991: capital utilization fee and
    depreciation

Sources: IMF (1994), World Bank (1995a)

That the causal relationship ought rather to be seen in reverse - because of the cessation of foreign economic aid expenditure had to be drastically reduced - does not detract from the adjustment effort. The stabilization policy was successful primarily because the structural and macroeconomic reform processes led to low inflation and high growth rates from 1992/93 and the results were therefore of the kind normally achieved under typical structural adjustment programs only on the basis of strict conditionality and external financial contributions.

Table 4: Aggregate savings and investment ratios (% of GDP)								
	1989[a]	1990	1991	1992	1993	1994	1995	1996[a]
Investment ratio	10.0	11.7	15.1	17.0	24.9	25.5	27.1	29.5
Savings ratio (domestic savings)	2.0	7.4	13.1	16.3	17.4	16.9	17.1	17.7
Current account deficit (foreign savings)	-8.0	-4.3	-2.0	-0.7	-7.5	-8.6	-10.0	-11.9
[a] estimate								
Sources: IMF (1994), World Bank (1995a), General Statistical Office (1995)								

Indebtedness and External Financing

Until 1990 the external financing of the current account deficit, or the national budget, had been made possible primarily by the accumulation of arrears, i.e. involuntary loans from trading partners, especially in the CMEA. As Table 5 shows, few of these loans were serviced by Vietnam.

While the situation as regard debts in transfer roubles has remained unchanged,[8] Vietnam is again capable of the ongoing servicing of debts in convertible currency following a bilateral rescheduling agreement with Japan in 1992 and agreements on the rescheduling of public debts reached with the Paris Club in 1993 and of private debts reached with the London Club in 1996. The financing of the current account deficit, which has been rising again since 1992, thus has a sounder basis than before, especially as new financial sources which are to account for most external financing in the medium term have become effective since 1993: foreign direct investment and concessionary credits from bi- and multilateral public donors. The Vietnamese government expects each of these two sources to provide about US$ 1 billion p.a. in the medium term, which, at a GDP of about US$ 24 billion (1996), would enable a current account deficit of almost 10 % of GDP and investments of more than 25 % of GDP to be financed (see Table 4). However, as the two sources have fulfilled expectations in terms only of pledges, but not of actual disbursements,[9] the current account deficit since 1993 appears rather too high. The IMF and World Bank, which agreed a structural adjustment program with the Vietnamese government in 1994 not least because of this financing deficit (see Chapter 8), advise against growing commercial indebtedness until the debts in transfer roubles have been settled.

Table 5: Foreign indebtedness					
	1989	1990	1991	1992	1993
Depts in convertible currency (m US$)	2,541	2,704	2,739	3,775	4,024
Debts in non-convertible currency (m transfer roubles)	10,790	11,077	10,774	10,867	10,935
Debt service ratio[a]					
- Debt service due	42.3	29.9	20.2	22.4	26.8
- Debt service paid	17.6	12.3	9.1	11.7	10.7
a Debt service as a percentage of exports of goods and services					
Source: IMF (1994)					

3.4   Integration into the World Economy

Until the late 1980s most of Vietnam's foreign trade was governed by bilateral protocols within the CMEA framework. It consisted largely of barter trade, an attempt being made to offset at least some of Vietnam's growing import requirements with exports of agricultural raw materials (coffee, rubber, etc.) and products of light industry (clothing, arts and crafts) and with the export of labor. From 1988 this trade declined and in 1991 finally collapsed altogether.

Vietnam found it easy to reorient its foreign trade primarily because of its favorable geographical situation. The economic isolation from the East Asian region had been so artificial that the change of environment in 1989, with the removal of trade restrictions and the adoption of a flexible exchange rate policy, was followed by a rapid switch of trade from the CMEA to the region or the world market almost as a matter of course. The speed with which the reorientation towards new trading partners was accomplished was due not least to a number of state-owned enterprises and trading organizations in the south of the country which had already established relations with enterprises in hard-currency countries before 1989 as part of their activities 'outside the plan' (Fforde 1993, p. 308).

Exports have since risen at two-digit rates, rice and oil, both new exports, initially accounting for more than a third of the total. Rice exports are the result of an increase in supply that occurred almost overnight in 1989. The oil exported comes from the Bac Ho field off the South Vietnamese coast, which was jointly developed with the Soviet Union and went on stream in the late 1980s.

Exports of manufactures have been rising since 1990 - starting from a very low base - and have the highest growth rate. Foreign direct investment makes no more than a small contribution, since it is only gradually beginning to move into the industrial sector. The lion's share comprises contract processing and production under license of footwear, clothing and toys, for example, where manufacture was able to begin immediately after Vietnam became more open in existing state-owned and private enterprises with little capital investment, usually on the basis of Chinese production and marketing know-how obtained from Taiwan, Hong Kong and Singapore. While the first increase in manufactured exports can thus be attributed to existing, unutilized capacities, the growth of exports in the next phase will be primarily due to foreign direct investment based on newly created capacities.

Table 6: Foreign trade (m US$)										
	1987	1988	1989	1990	1991	1992	1993	1994	1995	1996[a]
Exports	610	733	1.320	1.731	2.042	2.475	2.985	4.054	5.198	7.100
- oil	30	79	200	390	581	756	844	866	1.023	n.a.
- rice	-	-	316	272	225	300	363	429	496	n.a.
- seafood	113	124	133	220	285	302	427	489	430	n.a.
- coffee	24	25	31	25	74	86	110	234	564	n.a.
- industrial products	n.a.	101	137	175	267	598	1.085	n.a.	n.a.	n.a.
Imports	1.184	1.412	1.670	1.772	2.105	2.535	3.532	5.245	7.543	11.000
- oil products	n.a.	556	449	644	485	615	716	n.a.	724	n.a.
- fertilizers	n.a.	365	418	223	210	190	130	n.a.	554	n.a.
- machines and equipment	n.a.	245	169	213	338	801	1.090	n.a.	n.a.	n.a.
- vehicles	n.a.	57	86	89	79	312	615	n.a.	570	n.a.
Trade deficit	-575	-679	-350	-41	-63	-60	-547	-1.192	-2.345	-3.900
Sources: World Bank (1995a), Vietnam Investment Review										

The share of exports in GDP has risen to 25 - 30 % in the space of a few years, with more than two thirds going to the Asian region. In a very short period Vietnam has thus completed a regional integration process for which other countries - Indonesia, for example - needed far longer. Accession to the ASEAN alliance in July 1995 was therefore no more than a logical step, and one that - like the lifting of the US embargo the year before - removed barriers which had stood in the way of an almost natural trend for too long.

The financial constraints of the early 1990s automatically resulted in a balance of trade almost in equilibrium. Since 1993 imports have grown far more quickly than exports, reflecting the fairly liberal import regime in which tariffs average 15 %. This relatively pronounced openness, particularly to imports of consumer goods, is problematical not only for balance-of-payments reasons. Compared to the first phase of the industrialization of other countries in the region, there is practically no infant industry protection for the Vietnamese consumer goods industry. New product lines therefore have to be competitive in the world market from the outset, which is usually possible only if the latest, imported technologies are used. As the country's borders are largely open, there are, however, few alternatives. It is assumed that smuggling accounts for about a third of foreign trade - comprising foodstuffs and consumer goods for the most part - and that a more protectionist trade policy would increase this proportion.

In the case of primary commodities and intermediate products (steel, fertilizers, cement, paper, textile fibres) the import policy is far more protectionist. A system of quotas, import licenses and tariffs of up to 70 % protects the output primarily of the state-owned enterprises. Recently, joint ventures in new production lines (consumer electronics, vehicles, motorcycles) have also been protected against imports under a selective import substitution policy. The problem here is that this protection is afforded - under pressure from the manufacturers - for specific products and does not form part of a strategic concept, which ought, for example, to provide for the gradual removal of protection and for protection against imports to be linked to a strategy aimed at achieving international competitiveness.

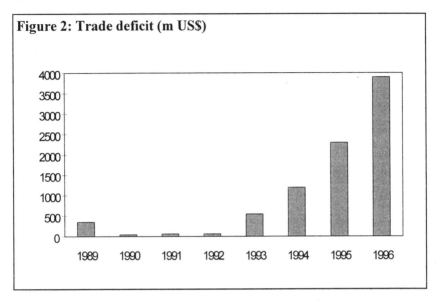

Figure 2: Trade deficit (m US$)

Now that the trade deficit has assumed critical proportions, as Figure 2 shows, the Vietnamese trade policy faces serious problems. For one thing, the short-term stabilization problem must be solved and the trade balance reduced to an acceptable deficit of US$ 2 - 3 billion. For another, Vietnam must prepare itself for integration into the ASEAN internal market, for which ambitious medium-term liberalization objectives have already been set.

In the short term the only option open to the government is a rapid increase in exports through the removal of all administrative export barriers, such as the licensing obligation which private exporters must still fulfill. There is also speculation about a lowering of the exchange rate of the dong, which has been nominally stable against the US dollar since 1993, i.e. it has risen in real terms. For the time being it will hardly be possible to abolish the licensing obligation and the quantitative restrictions on the import of primary commodities and intermediate products.

However, a restrictive import policy is in principle inconsistent with the liberalization obligations which Vietnam entered into on acceding to ASEAN in 1995 and to the ASEAN Free Trade Area (AFTA) in 1996. Within this framework internal tariffs are to be reduced to a maximum of 5 % by the year 2003 and quantitative restrictions are to be abolished, the only exceptions being a few 'sensitive' products. Although Vietnam has been granted an extension of the adjustment period until 2006, it faces the extremely ambitious prospect of having to compete within a decade in an ASEAN internal market where industry will in all likelihood develop rapidly in the next few years. While ASEAN internal trade in manufactures is not yet all that significant, this is likely to change in the next few years if only because of direct investment primarily from Japan, Korea, China and the USA geared to an ASEAN/10 market of 500 m inhabitants. Although the AFTA is not seeking common external tariffs, the requirements imposed by the WTO, which Vietnam would similarly like to join in the medium term, will also result in the world markets exerting heavy competitive pressure on Vietnam, which cannot be compared to the protectionist environment from which the Asian NICs benefited until well into the 1980s. The Vietnamese government does not yet appear to have fully appreciated the implications of this environment for its industrial policy.

3.5   Conclusions

The Vietnamese transformation policy was based on a blend of microeconomic liberalization and macroeconomic stabilization, which can certainly be described as abrupt for the period 1989-92. This policy, which reduced the rate of inflation drastically and led to GDP growth rates of between 5 and 9.5 %, was so successful primarily because of the immediate supply-side reaction. The peasant farms and state-owned enterprises had been prepared by the growing importance of markets and prices in the 1980s to the extent that the sudden abolition of central planning and the price reform were felt by most actors less as a shock than as a relief, the response being a corresponding rise in motivation and output.

In conjunction with the comprehensive reforms at micro level the consistent macroeconomic stabilization policy made a fundamental change in development policy possible without any major political or institutional changes being necessary. Although a wide range of institutional reforms was launched in the first half of the 1990s - they will be considered in greater depth in subsequent chapters - they had no impact during the first phase of transformation.

The change in development policy is reflected

– in the greater scope for growth which arose for Vietnam as a result of the reforms and is in principle enabling it to catch up with other Asian countries;

– in a sounder financial basis for the Vietnamese development process, with a higher rate of self-financing and thus less dependence on foreign aid, greater potential for government investment in infrastructure and the social sectors and the possibility of external funds being used for investment to a greater extent than before;

– in Vietnam's integration into the world economy and the opportunities it therefore has to benefit from the dynamism and division of labor in the region and participate in technological progress; however, this also means facing the risks and challenges that arise from international competition.

Forgoing the privatization of state-owned enterprises has not had any discernible adverse effects on the outcome of the first phase of transformation. The strategy of commercializing the state sector which was instead pursued initially had a stabilizing effect on tax revenue and the labor market. Why this policy should be adjusted in the medium term is explained in depth in Chapter 5. In Vietnam's case at least, the question posed in the World Bank's 1996 World Development Report ("From Plan to Market"), "Can privatization take a back seat in the early years of reform?" (World Bank 1996, p. 5.), can be answered with a cautious 'yes'.

4   Reform of the Financial Sector

4.1   Development Role of the Financial Sector

The Vietnamese economy's high growth rates in the first half of the 1990s were partly due to the increased use of underutilized capacities, inventory liquidation and easier access to imported inputs and consumer goods. In particular, the unexpected coincidence of restrictive financial policy and falling inflation on the one hand and high growth on the other can be interpreted as a reaction to the removal of repressive conditions that had restricted growth but given the Vietnamese economy a - one-time - efficiency gain.

This effect is also reflected in the high output-capital ratio on which growth was based. The growth of the GDP from 8 to 9.5 % p.a. in the period 1992-95 was achieved at an aggregate investment ratio that rose from 17 to 25 % of GDP (see Tables 2 and 4). The incremental capital-output ratio (ICOR)[1] was thus 2 - 2.5, which can be regarded as very favorable by international standards. Taking the average of other dynamic developing countries, the ratio of aggregate gross investment to additional output is 3 - 4.[2] If, then, Vietnam intends to achieve high growth rates in the longer term - the government's medium-term objective is growth of 8 - 10 % - the investment ratio must be increased further, given that capital-output ratios are likely to rise.[3] The decisive factor in this context, however, is how the rising investment is financed. If it is to be financed without excessive foreign indebtedness, domestic savings - by the state, enterprises and households - must be increased from the current 17 % to over 25 % of GDP. Another determining factor is the productivity of the capital projects financed: the higher the productivity, the lower the savings and investment ratios may be or the higher the aggregate growth rate will be.

The financial sector's main function for the Vietnamese development process is derived from this context:

- The banking system and the capital market play an important part in mobilizing savings and allocating capital efficiently. The significance of these functions rises as the complexity of the economy grows: the more the state's allocation decisions are transferred to a variety of microeconomic actors, the more important the financial markets' information function becomes.

– The central bank has the task of ensuring a suitable environment for an efficient banking system and the stability of the Vietnamese currency by employing monetary policy instruments.

The reform of numerous financial systems has shown that the two tasks - financing growth and stabilization - are inseparably linked and that abrupt attempts at liberalization may easily have destabilizing effects.[4] The transformation of the financial sector therefore requires a balanced mix of liberalization measures, measures to develop new institutions, sets of rules and instruments and macroeconomic stabilization measures. Arranging all these measures calls for extensive economic policy management skills because of the potential conflicts of objectives.

4.2   Structural Reform and Liberalization

Until 1988 the Vietnamese financial system consisted solely of the State Bank, which combined the functions of a central and commercial bank, and two special banks overseen by the State Bank, the Foreign Trade Bank (*Vietcombank*) and the Bank for Investment and Development of Vietnam (*BIDV*). These banks had the sole task of financing the national budget and state-owned enterprises. Credit allocation to enterprises was governed by the annual central credit plan. The branches of the State Bank and the two special banks were merely required to pass on funds without taking account of risks and credit periods. The interest rate policy was differentiated according to sector; real interest rates were negative, particularly at times of high inflation; lending rates were lower than deposit rates. As the State Bank was entirely under the control of the government, it had few opportunities to steer the money supply and credit formation. At regional level the State Bank's branches were exposed to the influence of the provincial governments, making the State Bank's role under the stabilization policy even more difficult. This extremely repressive financial system resulted in very little savings capital being mobilized, in a preference among savers for gold, dollars and physical assets, in the inflationary satisfaction of public sector borrowing requirements and in an inadequate supply of credit to the business community. The credit requirements of family firms and farms, the retail trade and informal trade and industry were met by the informal financial sector, i.e. money-lenders, friends and relatives and local savings and credit rings, such as the *hui* system, which is based on Chinese models (Wolff et al. 1995, pp. 25 f.).

When the transformation process began, the institutions of the banking system were extremely backward. There was no transparent accounting (balance sheets), no functioning payment system and no staff trained to international standards. The public had very little confidence in the banking system, and some of the country's leaders had very strong reservations about a commercialized banking system (Radke et al. 1992).

In 1988 the monobank system was abandoned for a two-tier financial system. The State Bank was to confine itself to performing the function of a central bank, but remained part of the government administration and continued to be subject to the government's sectorally differentiated control of interest rates and credit. The function of (state-owned) commercial banks was taken over by the two existing special banks and by the Agricultural Bank (*Agribank*) and the Bank for Trade and Industry (*Incombank*), both of which were separated from the State Bank. As an experiment, some state-owned enterprises also established joint stock banks.

Under the macroeconomic reform program of March 1989 real interest rates became positive for the first time; the sectoral differentiation of interest rates was abolished; non-state-owned enterprises and farms were also to have access to loans. In 1989, however, 80 % of *Agribank* loans and 90 % of *Incombank* loans still went to state-owned enterprises (Fforde 1995, p. 35).

It was not least because of this state monopolization of the banking system that the informal financial sector experienced a sharp upswing when the credit requirements of agriculture and small-scale trade and industry grew once the economic reform had begun. Newly established credit cooperatives, many of which were in fact private banks, tried to meet these credit requirements - including those of some state-owned enterprises - and were able to offer savers high interest rates because of the liberalized interest rate policy. When some were found to be operating snowball systems, there was a rush on the credit cooperatives in March 1990, leading to their collapse.

This development revealed a blatant lack of supervision and regulation in the banking system, which was not overcome until legislation was passed in 1990. With the *Law on the State Bank* the central bank was given far-reaching supervisory powers over the commercial banks. It was also assigned the typical functions of a central bank: the formulation and implementation of monetary and credit policy, the monitoring of credit creation, interest rate policy, minimum reserve policy and management of currency reserves. Its formal position as an organ of the government was left untouched. With a *Law on Commercial Banks and Credit Cooperatives* the four state-owned commercial banks and the private banks were formally granted the same conditions of competition. Barriers to market entry by domestic and foreign banks were lowered, although a separate *Decree on Foreign Banks* was passed to restrict the activities of foreign banks to certain areas of business - foreign trade financing and deposit business in foreign currencies.

The financial sector has since gained considerably in institutional width, although the state-owned banks still dominate:

– The four state-owned commercial banks have taken over virtually all the State Bank's credit business, including receivables from state-owned enterprises. The consequent burdens are substantial: according to World Bank estimates, irrecoverable debts owed to the state-owned commercial banks are equivalent to 25 % of total credit outstanding and twice their equity capital.[5] With a share of some 90 % of all banks' balance sheet totals, the state-owned commercial banks continued to dominate the banking sector in 1995.

- Some 50 non-state banks (joint stock banks), whose shareholders are mainly state-owned enterprises, ministries, the military and parastatal institutions (cooperative association, trade unions), were able to accumulate capital 'outside the plan' during the phase of growing commercialization of the government sector that began in the mid-1980s.

- A growing number of foreign banks, albeit with limited business opportunities; several joint venture banks and leasing companies; a number of branches of foreign investment banks.

- More than 200 predominantly rural credit cooperatives and share-holding banks, which were developed under a new law passed in 1993 on the initiative and under the supervision of the State Bank with the aim of placing rural financing on new foundations.

- An efficient money and foreign exchange market was developed as an interbank market from 1991 to 1993. The banks have since been able to trade their liquid resources among themselves on any official day of business without any interference from the State Bank.

- A securities market also began to emerge in the mid-1990s. Since 1992 the State Bank has been issuing government bonds, which have been largely absorbed by the commercial banks. A stock exchange on which bonds and shares are traded is planned for the late 1990s. An appreciable supply of securities cannot develop, however, until the state-owned enterprises are converted into corporations (equitization) and larger private enterprises begin to emerge.

Institutional diversification and slowly growing competition among the banks have led to a significant improvement in the efficiency of the banking system. Despite this, Vietnam is still a cash economy, with cash accounting for about 50 % of the M3 money supply (currency in circulation + short-term deposits + time deposits).[6] The mobilization of savings capital by the banking system - in terms of the ratio of time deposits to GDP - remained virtually unchanged at almost 20 % from 1989 to 1993 (China: about 40 %). The limited monetization of the economy is reflected in the financial deepening indicator (M3/GDP), which, at 25 - 30 %, is far lower than in other countries (China: about 100 %) (World Bank 1994, p. 11). It is estimated that less than 10 % of the population has so far had any contact with banks. This is mainly due to their lack of confidence in the Vietnamese currency and in a banking system which in the past was unfamiliar with the concept of banking secrecy and was unable to ensure that clients had access to their savings at any time. Added to this, the banks do not have enough branches in rural areas, and in the mid-1990s the payment system (transfers, cheques) is still antiquated and likely to improve appreciably only when a World Bank project pledged in 1995 (US$ 48 m for hardware and training) is completed.

4.3   The Central Bank's Monetary Policy

As inflation rates were high at the beginning of the reform process, the State Bank had no choice but to pursue a restrictive monetary and credit policy. This policy necessarily led to a limitation of the banking system's growth-financing role. Faced with the dilemma of the need for macroeconomic stabilization and the desire for rapid growth of the volume of credit, Vietnam has hitherto tended to opt for stability. This will also be necessary in the medium term because high capital inflows from abroad and lax monetary and fiscal policy in the past have left Vietnam with excess liquidity, which is difficult to control with the existing instruments of monetary policy. Monetary policy control is also made particularly difficult by the fact that a substantial proportion of financial assets is held in US dollars. Despite several years of a stable exchange rate between the dong and the US dollar, the replacement of the dollar with the dong is progressing extremely slowly. Besides the official capital inflows that appear in the balance of payments, there are extensive dollar holdings from unofficial transfers (some received from expatriate Vietnamese), although their potentially inflationary effect is curbed by high unofficial imports of goods, which constantly absorb a large proportion of these dollar holdings.

The State Bank's instruments are still heavily influenced by the planned-economy past to the extent that prices and quantities in the banking system - i.e. interest rates and volumes of credit - are still very largely determined by the State Bank's direct intervention. Such indirect instruments of monetary and credit policy as minimum reserve regulations, rediscount policy and open market policy, which leave it to the banks themselves to determine interest rates and volumes of credit, are only now being gradually developed.

Interest Rate Policy

Having been positive when the macroeconomic stabilization policy was launched, real interest rates fell below the rate of inflation again in 1990 and 1991. Since 1992 the interest rates on both deposits and loans have been positive in real terms.

Since 1990 the State Bank has done no more than impose ceilings on credit rates and lower limits on deposit rates. For all practical purposes the interest rate level is thus largely determined, since the banks need a margin of 7 - 8 % between deposit rates (for three-month deposits) and credit rates (for working capital) to cover their costs and make a profit. Savings deposits with longer maturities than three months are not as a rule accepted by the banks because the interest rate limits do not enable these funds to be used profitably.

Table 7: Selected interest rates in the banking system (% p.a.)							
	1989	1990	1991	1992	1993	1994	1995	1996
Deposit rates								
Short-term deposits								
• Households	60.0	28.8	25.2	12.0	8.4	8.4	8.4	4.8
• Enterprises	21.6	10.8	12.0	3.6	1.2	1.2	1.2	4.8
Savings deposits (3 months)								
• Households	84.0	48.0	42.0	24.0	16.8	16.8	16.8	6.6
• Enterprises	36.0	21.6	25.2	18.0	9.6	9.6	12.0	6.6
Savings deposits (6 months)								
•Households	-	-	-	-	-	20.4	20.4	16.8
•Enterprises	n.a.	-	-	18.0	12.0	12.0	12.0	n.a.
Savings deposits (12 months)	-	-	-	-	24.0	24.0	24.0	n.a.
Credit rates								
Agriculture (up to 12 months)	44.4	28.8	39.6	30.0	-	-	-	-
Industry and transport (up to 12 months)	45.6	32.4	36.0	24.0	-	-	-	-
Trade and tourism (up to 12 months)	46.8	34.8	44.4	32.4	-	-	-	-
Fixed assets (1-3 years)	-	9.6	9.6	21.6	14.4	20.4	20.4	16.2
Current assets (up to 12 months)	-	-	-	-	25.2	25.2	25.2	15.0
US$ loans	-	-	-	-	7.5	8.5	9.0	9.0
Rate of inflation	34.7	67.5	68.1	17.5	5.2	14.4	12.7	7.8
Sources: IMF (1994), p. 70; information provided by the State Bank								

In the early stages of transformation the State Bank set a wide range of deposit and credit rates, differentiated by sectors. Since 1993 credit rates have been differentiated only by maturity. The fact that the rates for long-term loans were well below the rates for short-term working capital loans until 1995 was due to the structure of the borrowers: almost all long-term loans were granted to state-owned enterprises (by the state-owned commercial banks). An attempt was thus being made to protect the state-owned enterprises themselves and the credit portfolio of the state-owned banks - with their large accounts receivable from the state-owned enterprises.

There are no plans for the moment for the complete deregulation of interest rates. Nor would this be appropriate to the present state of development of the financial system. It would encourage the already financially weak commercial banks to finance particularly risky investments at high interest rates (adverse selection). Heavily indebted borrowers would agree to any interest rate simply to survive (distress borrowing). High interest rates might also have a macroeconomically destabilizing effect by promoting inflation and short-term foreign capital inflows, as has occurred in some Latin American liberalization experiments (Chile, Argentina, Mexico).

Credit Policy

After interest rate policy, the direct influence on credit creation by the banking system is the second important monetary policy control instrument used by the State Bank. At quarterly intervals all the commercial banks have ceilings imposed on their credit business. These ceilings are guided by the limits on domestic credit creation agreed with the IMF under the structural adjustment program. The State Bank provides the four state-owned commercial banks, which account for about 90 % of the domestic volume of credit, with refinancing funds on terms which were differentiated by sectors until 1994 and so acted as an instrument of sectoral credit control. Since 1995 this differentiation has no longer applied: the four state-owned commercial banks receive funds from the State Bank at precisely the same interest rates as they charge their borrowers. Although the concessionary terms have meanwhile been removed, the allocation of certain refinancing facilities to the state-owned commercial banks, which specialize in given sectors, means that they still represent an instrument of sectoral credit control and the extension of outstanding loans to state-owned enterprises.

Credit creation on the basis of the savings deposits mobilized by the banking system itself is restricted by the minimum reserve policy as well as the credit ceilings. The State Bank adopts a two-pronged approach in this respect: it raises a minimum reserve on the deposits and also requires that cash held by the banks in excess of a certain limit be paid into a low-interest (1.2 % p.a.) State Bank account. Administrative problems with the calculation and enforcement of the banks' minimum reserve obligations have hitherto resulted in far greater use being made of this cash reserve to control liquidity in the banking system than the actual minimum reserve (World Bank 1994, p. 30). In all, the State Bank claims up to 20 % of the commercial banks' cash, sight and time deposits as reserves, while directly financing about a third of the credit allocated by the state-owned commercial banks with the aid of its refinancing facilities. Monetary and credit policy control is thus based on direct quantitative control, which, in view of the tight limits on their lending and the fixed interest rate structures, leaves the banks very little room for maneuver.

4.4   Credit Supply to the Business Community

State-owned enterprises

In 1995 the state-owned enterprises absorbed only about 50 % of the commercial banks' volume of credit. The four state-owned commercial banks are involved to varying degrees: while the *Bank for Investment and Development* still grants over 90 % of its loans to the state sector, the *Incombank* is now down to less than 50 % and the *Agribank* to less than 30 %. The non-state joint stock banks too give about half of their loans to private enterprises. The state-owned enterprises do, however, receive a disproportionately large share of medium- and long-term loans (with a life longer than three months), loans in foreign currency (US dollars) accounting for the largest proportion since 1993. Enterprises benefit from the low interest rates (about 9 % p.a.) and consider the currency risk relatively low, since the dong/US dollar exchange rate has not changed substantially since 1992.

The state-owned enterprises' extensive arrears continue to form a major burden for the state-owned commercial banks. As no valuation adjustments have to be made for these loans, the banks have no incentive to show these enterprises as being in default. This is particularly true where there is no prospect of the collateral being used. The usual procedure is to roll over such loans. Precisely how high the credit risks are is not therefore known. IMF and World Bank estimates put them at about 25 % of the state-owned commercial banks' assets. They are joined by risks arising from credit guarantees which the banks have provided for state-owned enterprises borrowing abroad and from as yet unpaid debts owed by one state-owned enterprise to another, which may lead to a chain reaction affecting the banks.

Until this problem of old debts has been solved, there will be strict limits to the commercial banks' room for maneuver and to their chances of operating profitably. The government is obviously inclined to solve the problem by gradually improving the commercial banks' portfolios. However, this would at least require the scale of the loans in default to be revealed by detailed auditing and the necessary valuation adjustments to be gradually undertaken. The World Bank similarly prefers a gradualistic approach to the rehabilitation of the banking system, combined with a policy of actively promoting the establishment of new private banks in the market. It does not believe that easing the burden of loans in default on the banks - and possibly the state-owned enterprises - too quickly would in itself change attitudes on lending and in some transforming economies would lead to repeated recapitalization of the banks ("Beware of recapitalizing banks") (World Bank 1996, p. 102). Recently, not only the state-owned banks but also some newly established joint stock banks have been accused of incorrect assessments of risks inherent in real estate transactions and short-term trade loans.[7] It is evident that the promotion of competition in the banking system must be accompanied by the establishment of appropriate regulatory and supervisory mechanisms, since otherwise destabilizing developments may quickly occur.

Rural Financing

With the decollectivization of agriculture, the demand for credit from family farms had risen sharply. It fell to the *Agribank* to meet at least some of this demand. In the mid-1990s it remains the most important financial institution for rural areas, not least because of its relatively dense network of branches. The state-owned enterprises' share of the *Agribank*'s credit portfolio fell from 95 % in 1991 to 65 % in 1992 and less than 30 % in 1995. One reason for the rapid decline in lending to state-owned enterprises was that a substantial proportion of the usually 'provincially managed' state-owned enterprises in the rural areas were declared bankrupt or liquidated in the course of re-registration in 1992 (see section 5.1). For the *Agribank* this meant, on the one hand, a heavy burden of loans in default but, on the other hand, greater freedom to provide loans for agriculture, primarily on the basis of the State Bank's rediscount lines, since very little savings capital was at first mobilized in the rural areas.

The *Agribank* increasingly relies on group loans and such intermediaries as cooperatives, the farmers' association or the women's association to reduce transaction costs in the small loan business. The allocation of the credit portfolio is still heavily influenced by the planned economy, since the distribution of available credit funds from headquarters to the branches, sectors and individual borrowers tends to be determined by political, and especially social, factors rather than profitability criteria. Something of an adjustment of this development bank function of the *Agribank* might result from the fact that the *Bank of the Poor* established by the *Agribank* in 1996 is taking over the small loan programs, which are permanently in need of subsidization, and endeavoring to reach the poorest target groups in the rural areas with international development aid. Reaching these target groups is difficult mainly because the *Agribank* normally requires collateral in the form of houses and land use rights, even in the case of group loans. In many cases, however, land use rights in particular have still to be finally clarified even now, several years after decollectivization.

Almost all the loans granted by the *Agribank* are short-term, the interest payable by rural borrowers usually being somewhat higher than the upper limits prescribed by the State Bank, mainly because of the involvement of intermediaries. While the interest rate on short-term loans from 1993 to 1995 was about 25 % (see Table 7), peasant households normally had to pay 30 - 35 % (World Bank 1994, p. 65).

As the *Agribank* comes nowhere near to satisfying the demand for loans in rural areas, despite these high interest rates, the informal financial market continues to meet much of this demand. Since the credit cooperatives, which were largely unregulated and must therefore be regarded as having formed part of the informal financial market, collapsed almost completely in the early 1990s, private loans and money lenders have met most of the demand for credit at interest rates about two to three times higher than those charged by the *Agribank*. These loans are often used, however, solely for the short-term interim financing of formal loans, which are of too short a duration to bridge the agricultural production cycles completely.

It can be assumed, however, that the gradual expansion of the *Agribank*'s small loan business was enough to reduce informal financing. This purpose is also served by a system of credit cooperatives (*People's Credit Funds*) newly created in 1993, which, apart from a few small semi-private rural shareholding banks, are the only alternative to the *Agribank* in the rural areas. The *People's Credit Funds* and the private rural banks have so far been able to mobilize only a small volume of savings capital, principally because of the State Bank's restrictive interest rate policy, and therefore depend on refinancing funds from the State Bank or the *Agribank*. These new financial institutions seem particularly suitable for rural financing mainly because, being so close to their clients, their collateral requirements are less stringent. Dissatisfaction with the credit cooperatives in the past, however, means that considerable confidence-building efforts will be needed if more local savings capital is to be mobilized in the medium term. Given the strong influence of the State Bank and *Agribank* during its start-up phase, it remains to be seen whether an autonomous system of rural banking with regional liquidity equalization and a central auditing and deposit guarantee system actually emerges from the *People's Credit Funds*, as their statutes provide (Wolff et al. 1995, pp. 22 ff.).

International development cooperation is involved in rural financing with a whole series of credit lines, which are channeled through the *Agribank*. The World Bank and Asian Development Bank alone have pledged credit lines amounting to more than US$ 150 m, enabling longer-term loans (9 - 12 months) to be granted on a significant scale for the first time. More important than these capital flows from outside, however, would appear to be the development of local credit creation based on domestic savings, which depend primarily on the monetary stability and consistent institutional development of the financial sector.

At the other end of the development cooperation scale many international NGOs are trying to contribute to direct poverty alleviation in rural areas with target-group-oriented credit funds. Initial experience with these approaches has not been very encouraging, however, since it has so far proved impossible to develop these funds into sustainable financial institutions (ibid., pp. 26 f.). In view of their limited spillover effects these approaches have so far had no significant impact on the development of the financial system.

Industry and Small and Medium-sized Enterprises

The supply of short-term credit from the banking system to the non-agricultural private sector, which largely consists of small firms, has improved significantly since the reform began. The state *Incombank* and the newly established joint stock banks used about half of their portfolio to finance the private sector in the mid-1990s. Various surveys of enterprises have shown that in 1995 some 10 % of small firms and two thirds of medium-sized firms obtained loans from the formal banking sector (Meier / Pilgrim 1995, Wolff et al. 1995).

While informal financial sources still play an important role, particularly in the trade sphere, small and medium-sized industrial firms depend largely on financing from their own resources and family loans despite the improved supply of credit. The banking system has so far been able to meet very little of the demand for longer-term investment financing. Large private firms have access to foreign currency loans, with a high currency risk to match; others take advantage of the possibility of extending short-term loans several times.

Besides the short-term structure of their deposits, the main reason for the banks' reluctance to finance investment in the longer term is the unclear legal position with regard to the assertion and enforcement of claims against creditors and the cautious policy on collateral that the banks therefore adopt. Although the Bank Law permits real estate, movable assets, land use rights and third-party guarantees to be accepted as security, the unclear and frequently amended provisions on land use rights and the difficulty of obtaining enforceable legal title from the appropriate courts of arbitration result, in practice, in the banks accepting only buildings as security. The whole volume of credit available to the private sector is thus limited to the value of existing buildings that can be accepted as security - usually only 50 - 70 % of their market value. The fact that land cannot be used as collateral for loans in Vietnam is thus a disadvantage not only for the individual borrower but also for the economy as a whole, since the level of private investment that can be financed by the banking system is kept unnecessarily low.

While in the medium term the financing of enterprises from their own resources must be joined by a significant improvement in long-term capital injections through the banking system to solve the problem of financing the private trade and industry sector, the **securities market** will play a growing role in the longer term. The opening of a stock exchange was originally planned for 1996/97, but had to be deferred because of the hesitant implementation of the equitization program for the state-owned enterprises (see section 5.1). In July 1996 the first state-owned enterprise to be transformed into a joint stock company issued convertible bonds to the value of US$ 5 m and so became the first example of a foreign portfolio investment (Far Eastern Economic Review, 29 August 1996, p. 61). Only when a considerable number of state-owned and private enterprises have been constituted in the form of joint stock companies that meet international accounting and balance-sheet requirements will trade in company shares be appropriate and possible. An institutional structure of auditing and investment firms with the specialist know-how needed for this process is emerging, primarily in Ho Chi Minh City. The fact that the government is delaying this development for political reasons has also resulted in international portfolio capital - in the form of a number of international *Vietnam funds* - so far finding very few investment opportunities in Vietnam.

4.5   Conclusions - Need for Further Reforms

The development of the Vietnamese financial sector in the first half of the 1990s was characterized by cautious liberalization, the gradual transformation of existing institutions and the creation of new ones and the general primacy of stability. This cautious, gradualistic approach to reforms has proved successful on the whole, because it has enabled processes of macroeconomic destabilization to be avoided and the financial sector's most important asset - confidence in the stability of the currency and the banking system - to be gradually improved.[8]

Vietnam is nonetheless still far from having a modern market-economy financial system: only the beginnings of market-economy instruments are being used for monetary policy control; the banking system is still not differentiated enough and is dominated by the undercapitalized state-owned commercial banks; the burgeoning private sector has little access to medium- and longer-term financial resources.

The role played by the **State Bank** in maintaining stability has been very much strengthened by the fact that it has not been expected to finance the national budget directly since 1992. Although it cannot, as part of the government, pursue an independent monetary policy - which would, moreover, be hardly conceivable in the current political environment - the State Bank has since been able to impose consistent liquidity and credit limits, which has led to a decline in the rate of inflation. It will be some time before the money and capital markets are sufficiently developed for the State Bank to be able to switch to an open market policy as an alternative to the present direct control of the money supply. Similarly, the liberalization of interest rates will be possible only when the banking system has a sounder basis of capital resources.

Relieving the State Bank of the financing of the national budget does mean, however, that the banking system is burdened with the debts of the state-owned enterprises. This legacy of the planned economy is slowing the development of the banking system considerably. Rapid recapitalization is problematical for the reasons given above. However, at least the **bank supervision** function, which is performed by the State Bank, should be strengthened. The state-owned banks need clear rules on the adjustment of the value of loans in default. The same regulations on capital resources and accounting methods should apply to private and state-owned banks.

The continued development of the **legal framework** for the financial system will depend not least on the speed with which the principle of the rule of law generally gains acceptance in Vietnam and the legal rules that are created are enforced in the administration and the courts. This is particularly true of the clear definition of property rights and the judicial enforcement of claims. Although a *civil code* and a *bankruptcy law* have meanwhile entered into force and can act as the basis, for example, of legislation on cheques and bills of exchange or legal rules on the use of real securities, it will take some considerable time for the Vietnamese (socialist) legal tradition of out-of-court arbitration proceedings to give way to a completely new legal approach, despite the existence of new legal rules.

The reform of the financial sector in a transforming economy primarily means **institution-building**. Apart from the decision of principle to dissolve the monobank system, the progress made in this respect has been unspectacular because the transformation process essentially occurred on the basis of the existing institutions and with the existing staff complement. In these circumstances, however, the gradual modernization of the State Bank and commercial banks through the introduction of new technologies and instruments and above all the training of staff - usually with the support of development aid and cooperation with international banks - was vital if the reform was to be undertaken. Innumerable minor institutional measures, which, taken together, are nonetheless changing the system, are just as important for the transformation process as the macroeconomic and regulatory decisions of principle. Particular reference can be made in this context to important institutions that complement the banking system and have emerged in recent years: a deposit security fund, which will, however, become effective only after a few years of accruing capital; an association of banks to engage in dialogue with the State Bank and the government; the bank supervision already mentioned and a structure of private auditing firms. They are joined by the development of new bank training centers and the institutional links forged with the international financial system through the creation of a network of international correspondent banks, for example; the connection to the international SWIFT payment system and the establishment of a modern foreign exchange trading system in the State Bank. As a result of this institutional reinforcement and differentiation the transformation of the financial system is gaining some momentum of its own. Beyond the reach of political control by the government or the party, institutional self-control of the system is developing and propelling modernization from within.

The sequencing of the reform of the financial sector can on the whole be described as successful: basic regulatory reforms from 1988 to 1990, consistent stabilization since 1992, cautious liberalization and institutional reforms over the whole period. Yet the banking system's contribution to economic growth has so far tended to be modest. For reasons of monetary and institutional stability the monetary policy has restrained financial intermediation by the banking system. The political decision of principle to solve the state-owned enterprises' debt problem through the banking system rather than the national budget has imposed a further restriction on the banks' room for maneuver. That high rates of economic growth have nonetheless been achieved is an indication of relatively substantial self-financing potential in the real sector.

The development of the real sector has, moreover, had major repercussions for the financial sector: a successful reform of the state-owned enterprises is facilitating the recapitalization of the state-owned commercial banks and laying the foundations for the domestic securities market; rising demand for financial services is emerging from a dynamic private sector. Chapter 5 reviews some of the main problems associated with the development of the real sector.

5   Reform of the Enterprises

5.1   State-owned Enterprises

Before the economic reform began, state-owned enterprises in Vietnam were regarded as the pivot of the central planning system and the basis of economic development, and especially industrialization. While nationalization and collectivization in agriculture were never entirely successful, eventually failing during the 1980s, state-owned enterprises in the non-agricultural sectors were the dominant form of organization besides cooperatives and family firms. From 1976 to 1989 the number of state-owned enterprises rose from about 7,000 to 12,000. However, only about a quarter were industrial enterprises. Compared to other transforming economies, Vietnam's state sector, and especially the state industrial sector, was fairly small: in 1986 the state sector (excluding public administration) contributed 28 % of GDP, the state industrial sector 16.9 % (Table 8). Only about 15 % of all employees worked in the state sector, two thirds of them in state-owned enterprises (Table 9).

The core of the state-owned enterprises, accounting for about half of all employees, is formed by some 1,500 centrally managed enterprises. Each is the responsibility of a ministry (not only the industrial sector ministries but also the defense and home affairs ministries), which in the past controlled the enterprises directly or through an intermediate level of sectoral enterprise unions or integrated plants.

Table 8: State and non-state shares of gross domestic product, by sectors of the economy (%)

	1986	1987	1988	1989	1990	1991	1992	1993	1994
Total	100.0	100.0	100.0	100.0	100.0	100.0	100.0	100.0	100.0
- state	37.6	35.8	32.5	33.2	32.5	33.3	36.2	39.2	40.2
- non-state[a]	62.4	64.2	67.5	66.8	67.5	66.7	63.8	60.8	59.8
Agriculture and forestry	36.4	39.2	44.8	40.8	37.5	39.5	33.0	28.8	27.7
- state	1.8	1.8	1.5	1.3	1.0	1.1	0.9	0.7	0.7
- non-state	34.6	37.4	43.3	39.5	36.4	38.4	32.1	28.0	26.9
Industry	27.7	27.1	22.6	20.3	20.2	20.8	22.6	22.6	23.0
- state	16.9	16.5	13.6	12.4	12.3	13.4	15.1	15.4	15.9
- non-state	10.8	10.6	9.0	7.9	7.7	7.4	7.5	7.2	7.1
Construction	2.8	2.5	2.8	3.8	3.8	4.0	5.6	7.4	7.6
- state	1.8	1.7	1.7	2.1	2.0	1.8	2.5	3.7	3.5
- non-state	1.0	0.8	1.1	1.7	1.9	2.2	3.1	3.7	4.1
Services	33.0	31.0	29.8	35.0	38.6	35.7	38.8	41.2	41.6
- state	17.0	15.7	15.7	17.3	17.1	17.0	17.6	19.3	20.0
thereof: public admi-nistration	9.5	9.7	9.5	10.2	8.5	8.8	8.8	10.5	10.7
- non-state	16.0	15.3	14.1	17.7	21.5	18.7	21.2	21.9	21.6

a   The non-state sector comprises cooperatives and private enterprises

Sources: General Statistical Office (1995), World Bank (1995a)

The management of the remaining state-owned enterprises is decentralized: they are run by provincial, district or local authorities. In the past they formed part of the centrally planned system, but came under the local people's committees, the quasi-owners. Clearly, the number and size of locally managed enterprises play an important role in terms of the economic and political significance of a province. During the war in particular, but afterwards too, the locally managed state-owned enterprises enjoyed a relatively high degree of autonomy, if only because communications were poor. For the centrally and locally managed enterprises central planning was, moreover, confined to setting important production-related plan targets and providing subsidized inputs. Beyond this, there was no systematic central control of the development of the state-owned enterprises. The mere fact that the centrally managed enterprises came under the various specialist ministries, which were not prepared to share their power of control with a central authority, the State Planning Commission, for example, made this impossible.

Table 9:	Employees in the state and non-state sectors (1,000)									
	1986	1987	1988	1989	1990	1991	1992	1993	1994	1995
Total population	61.109	62.452	63.727	64.774	66.233	67.774	69.405	71.026	72.510	73.959
Gainfully employed	27.398	27.968	28.478	28.941	30.294	30.974	31.819	32.716	33.669	34.208
Private sector	3.641	3.594	3.768	5.390	6.459	9.759	10.215	29.715	30.735	31.205
Cooperatives[a]	19.730	20.283	20.658	19.750	20.414	18.071	18.629	n.a.	n.a.	n.a.
State sector	4.027	4.091	4.052	3.801	3.421	3.144	2.975	2.923	2.934	3.003
- administration	1.369	1.383	1.359	1.295	1.340	1.269	1.242	1.250	1.232	1.262
- state-owned enterprises	2.658	2.708	2.693	2.506	2.046	1.840	1.733	1.704	1.696	1.741

[a] The figures on employment in the cooperative sector are too high throughout, especially after the de facto dissolution of the agricultural production cooperatives in 1989. From 1993 employees of the cooperatives are added to the private sector.

Sources: General Statistical Office (1995), IMF (1996), p. 50

Most of the state-owned enterprises are small or medium-sized. The latest available figures on the industrial sector show 275 of the 2,268 centrally and locally managed state-owned industrial enterprises to have more than 500 employees. The remaining 2,000 have an average of 130 (World Bank 1995a, p. 100). While the large enterprises are mostly centrally managed and form part of the strategic oil, coal, chemical, transport and fertilizer sectors, the provincial and local authorities tend to control the smaller firms in light industry.

As mentioned in Chapter 2, the state-owned enterprises had enjoyed some autonomy as regards production 'outside the plan' since the early 1980s. Their managers learnt, on the one hand, how to persuade the central authorities to set them the lowest possible plan targets for their output and give them the highest possible subsidies for their inputs and, on the other hand, how to seize the opportunities presented by the informal markets. With the introduction of even greater freedom in 1987 - with regard to production, investment, financing, pricing and personnel - many enterprises tried to diversify their activities into the consumer goods sector because it offered the best marketing prospects. However, the pricing policy shock therapy of 1989 and the end of transfers from the national budget imposed a hard budget constraint on the state-owned enterprises for the first time and was followed by a drastic adjustment process.

Having fallen slightly in 1989, production by the state-owned enterprises has risen steadily since 1990. However, the workforce shrank by about 30 % - more than 800,000 people - from 1989 to 1992 (Table 9). These aggregate figures reflect the collapse of numerous enterprises, most of them small and locally managed. The government tried to help the enterprises in difficulty by relaxing the credit policy. After inflation flared up again, however, this policy was rapidly readjusted (see Chapter 3).

Consolidation of the State-owned Enterprise Sector

In 1990 the first formal legal foundations for the existence of state-owned enterprises were laid by decree, requiring all state-owned enterprises to re-register in subsequent years. In principle, only economically viable enterprises were to be re-registered. A debt commission was set up to determine the scale of the enterprises' arrears and oversee the liquidation of those with excessive debts. By the end of this streamlining process in 1994 some 6,000 enterprises had been re-registered. About 2,000 were liquidated, about 4,000 merged with other enterprises. As most of the enterprises wound up were small,[1] the state sector continued to carry the same weight in the Vietnamese economy: a decline in the state share of GDP in the latter half of the 1980s was followed by a steady recovery from 1990/91 (Table 8). While the state sector no longer plays any part in agriculture, where there are only a few state farms and state trading firms left, it carried greater weight in the industrial sector in 1994 than before the reform, accounting for about two thirds of industrial output. A major factor in this context, however, is the considerable rise in production by the oil and electricity enterprises, which are 100 % state-owned. But state-owned enterprises were also able to maintain or increase their share in other sectors: metal-working 91 %, electronics 73 %, chemicals 75 %, construction materials 65 %, cellulose and paper 73 %, food-processing 67 % and textiles 66 %.[2] The strong position of the state-owned enterprises in these sectors is also reflected in the important function they perform in the financing of the national budget, which has already been emphasized in Chapter 3. As Table 10 shows, the abolition of subsidies to the state-owned enterprises has been only partly offset by bank loans. Their cash flow has thus changed fundamentally for the better as a result of the reform.

It is difficult to say whether these payment flows also reflect greater profitability of the capital invested in the state-owned enterprises because their accounting, and above all the valuation of their assets, is not transparent. The sharp drop in numbers employed, however, has led to a significant increase in their productivity.

It must be assumed that for fiscal reasons transfers to the budget, three quarters of which consist of taxes and one quarter of depreciation and service of capital, are calculated as high as possible to the enterprises' disadvantage. As income determination is not transparent, the taxation of profits is, in the final analysis, a matter for negotiation. The same is true of the level of depreciation funds transferred to the budget. The enterprises were, moreover, able to retain them from 1989 to 1992. Thereafter they had to be transferred to the state again at 100 % (Fforde 1995, p. 88). This procedure can be interpreted as a necessary hard budget constraint. For market-economy enterprises, i.e. enterprises competing internationally, it would, however, mean substantial asset erosion. If the state-owned enterprises were privatized or fully exposed to competition, the transfers to the budget would undoubtedly have to be far lower.

Table 10: Financial relations between state-owned enterprises, banks and the national budget (% of GDP)

	1987	1988	1989	1990	1991	1992	1993	1994
Transfers from state-owned enterprises to the budget	10.8	7.9	8.4	8.6	8.1	10.8	11.8	12.1
thereof: oil levies	-	-	1.1	2.0	2.8	3.8	3.8	3.1
Budget transfers to state-owned enterprises	7.9	8.5	4.8	2.6	1.0	0.9	0.6	0.5
Balance	3.0	-0.6	3.6	6.0	7.0	9.9	11.2	11.6
New bank loans to state-owned enterprises	9.6	9.2	7.1	4.1	5.0	3.0	2.2	2.4
Net transfer from the budget and banks to state-owned enterprises	6.6	9.7	3.5	-2.0	-2.0	-6.9	-8.9	-9.2

Source: IMF (1996), p. 13

Most of the large centrally managed state-owned enterprises have a monopolistic position in the market. Their financial situation is thus improved by monopoly rents. They also receive indirect subsidies, which are not shown in the budget: concessionary credit terms as before, the availability of large industrial sites free of charge and privileged access to foreign trade licenses. Many have also shown loans in default in their balance sheets - including some of the 10 billion transfer roubles owed by Vietnam (see Chapter 3) - which are a potential threat to their financial stability.

On balance, the state-owned enterprises' positive financial position is fragile. Important though the transfers to the budget may be for macroeconomic stability, they are at risk if market-economy reforms, combined with more competition and a reduction of indirect subsidies to state-owned enterprises, continue. The sustainability of the strategy adopted of stabilizing the state sector is thus by no means ensured. Financial consolidation does not mark the end of the reform of the state-owned enterprises. The IMF and World Bank in particular are pressing for their privatization. Under agreements on the implementation of a structural adjustment program financially supported by the World Bank and IMF the Vietnamese government committed itself in 1994[3]

–   to dividing the state-owned enterprises into strategic and non-strategic enterprises,

–   to converting the non-strategic enterprises into joint stock companies and making them subject to the existing Enterprise Law, which has hitherto applied only to non-state-owned enterprises, and

–   to creating a separate legal basis for the strategic enterprises, which will remain in the state sector, establishing a supervisory authority and submitting these enterprises to internationally standard rules of accountancy.

Internal differences in the CPV about the continuation of the reform of the state-owned enterprises have resulted in only some of these commitments being honored. Thus, although the parliament passed a *Law on the State-owned Enterprises* and a supervisory department was installed in the Finance Ministry in 1995, conversion into joint stock companies has been very slow.

In fact, a pilot program launched in 1993 for the equitization of 19 small and medium-sized state-owned enterprises has been virtually halted. Equitization means conversion into joint stock companies or limited liability companies, with some 20 % of the shares being offered to the workforce (who can obtain interest-free loans for the purpose) and at least 20 % remaining the property of the state. By the end of 1996 only 6 state-owned enterprises had been converted in this way: a transport company belonging to the Transport Ministry, a refrigeration equipment manufacturer previously owned by Ho Chi Minh City, a footwear factory formerly the property of the Ministry for Light Industry and three other, relatively small enterprises. In the case of the other candidates for conversion either the complex valuation problems could not be solved or the workforce and management opposed the conversion because they believed they would lose their jobs or privileges. Furthermore, most 'owners' of state-owned enterprises at central and local level have no interest in the conversion of profitable enterprises. Lacking the pressure of a comprehensive reform concept from the party and government, the equitization program, which is voluntary, has therefore not yet been able to achieve its objectives.

Another government program, which tends to run counter to the agreements with the IMF and World Bank, is the establishment of sectoral general corporations in which many of the state-owned enterprises are to be consolidated and evade direct interference from sectoral ministries and provincial governments. In 1995 14 general corporations were established in the energy, coal, oil and gas, steel, cement, textile, mechanical engineering, posts and telecommunications, paper, air and sea transport, coffee, tobacco and rubber sectors. As the government sees it, these vertically and horizontally integrated general corporations form the nucleus of Vietnam's continued industrialization. Observers already see them as "the Vietnamese answer to the Korean *Chaebols*" (Gates 1995a).

The choice of sectors reveals the government's belief that state-owned enterprises should continue to operate in industries in which there are already private enterprises in considerable numbers. This intention is further endorsed by the report of the CPV leadership to the 8th Party Congress in June 1996, which held out the prospect of the state sector - together with the cooperatives - contributing 60 % of GDP by the year 2020 (Vietnam Investment Review, 15-21 April 1996, p. 1), a clear declaration of support for the dominance of the state over the private sector.

The danger associated with the formation of the general corporations is that, given the weight they carry, competition will continue to be restricted in much of industry. The strategic role allotted to these conglomerates would undoubtedly be reflected in privileged access to capital and other concessions. Cross-subsidization of weaker enterprises under the roof of the general corporations might give rise to structures more appropriate to the old integrated plants that have been dissolved since the late 1980s than to modern, internationally competitive enterprises.

Commercialization and Quasi-privatization

Besides the official efforts to restructure the state-owned enterprise sector that have been described above, there are clear signs of a move towards increased commercialization of the state sector. The most important determinant in this respect is foreign direct investment. Almost all the partners of foreign investors are state-owned enterprises. Most of the larger state-owned enterprises have succeeded - partly because of their monopolistic position in some markets - in attracting foreign partners, not only in their traditional production sectors but also in areas of business completely new to them, mainly in the real estate, tourism and service sectors. For some state-owned enterprises joint ventures are a welcome opportunity to acquire capital, modern technologies and know-how and to modernize their production lines. The few modern production plants established in Vietnam in the first half of the 1990s are nearly all joint ventures. For another, and presumably the larger, group of state-owned enterprises joint ventures mean earnings and investment potential that will enable some to diversify and many others simply to survive.

In many joint ventures the Vietnamese partner's contribution merely consists of land or the long-term land use right assigned to the state-owned enterprise by the state. This contribution is often set at 30 - 40 % of the joint venture's capital stock, from which the Vietnamese partner derives corresponding profit shares. As joint ventures are usually limited to 20 - 25 years, this construction, which is also common in China, is more in the nature of a license or concession to the foreign partner, with the profit share as the license fee, than a long-term joint venture. Given the prospect of the foreign share being transferred to the Vietnamese partner on the expiry of the joint venture contract, this variant of the diversification and modernization of state-owned enterprises is viewed more favorably by many in the party than the emergence of private capitalist enterprises, i.e. private companies over a certain size. It enables the state-owned enterprises to accumulate 'capital of their own', which they have greater or lesser freedom to dispose of, the further removed they are from the influence of central government. In this way the independence of the management of state-owned enterprises is growing. Where enterprises still depend on political protection, there is interdependence - especially at local level - between political decision-makers and the management of state-owned enterprises, which does not differ substantially from the traditional symbiosis of politics and the economy, although it is becoming far more commercial today.

Another, no less common variant of the commercialization of state-owned enterprises can be called quasi-privatization. As in other transforming economies, this consists of more or less spontaneous processes of uncontrolled redistribution of the assets of state-owned enterprises or of private gain from the use of state assets. This is often achieved through interaction with private enterprises, which, for example, use the land and machinery of a state-owned enterprise at a favorable price, obtain loans or foreign trade licenses through the enterprise and so make, under government protection, profits that are transferred to the parent company or its management in part officially, but also unofficially in many cases.

While both forms of commercialization described above result in growing room for maneuver and development opportunities for the state-owned enterprise, they also make the dividing line between public and private increasingly fluid. Evidently, it is now widely believed in Vietnam that the capital which state-owned enterprises have themselves accumulated does not belong to the state, but to the enterprises themselves, i.e. the management and workforce, and to private informal shareholders (Probert and Young 1995, pp. 515 f.).

There is likely to be little interest at present in clear general rules on property rights in the state sector since many government institutions and decision-makers at central and regional level benefit from the present situation. Ministries, the military, provincial authorities and local administrations derive a growing proportion of their revenue from semi-private business activities, usually associated with state-owned enterprises. Such involvement typically consists of the establishment of a private enterprise or joint venture with a state-owned enterprise's 'own capital'.

These interests at the lower and middle decision-making levels match the government's interest in the continuation of high transfers from state-owned enterprises to the budget and the party's interest in seeing the state own a large share of the economy. In these circumstances, comprehensive privatization of state-owned enterprises is unlikely to begin in the foreseeable future. The Finance Ministry, which has been formally responsible for administering the assets of state-owned enterprises since the beginning of 1995, is endeavoring to revive the equitization program and to convert 100 - 200 enterprises into shareholding companies each year by this method (Vietnam Investment Review, April 1996). For this, however, there would need to be a clear political declaration of intent from the government, which it has yet to deliver.

Since the beginning of the economic reform the Vietnamese government has failed to pursue a clear strategy for the transformation of the

state-owned enterprise sector. All that was clear was that it would prefer a gradualistic reform process to rapid privatization. An early increase in the autonomy of the state-owned enterprises, the introduction
of a not entirely stringent, but nonetheless effective hard budget constraint, accompanied by the continued existence of some privileges,
and commercialization through joint ventures and quasi-privatization
have in the end proved to be a generally successful strategy for the first
phase of transformation: the state-owned enterprises have become financially stable; the reduction of employment has been completed
since 1992; the enterprises are expanding on the basis of market-
oriented output.

Still largely open, on the other hand, is the question of relevance to
development strategy whether the state-owned enterprises can in the
longer term actually form the basis of an internationally competitive
Vietnamese industry, as the comparison with the Korean *Chaebols*
suggests. There are certainly examples of state-owned enterprises oc-
cupying a strong position in other dynamic Asian countries. Thus 19 of
the 50 largest enterprises in Taiwan in 1981 and 20 of the 50 largest in
Korea in 1972 were state-owned. In Taiwan state-owned enterprises
still accounted for about half of all investment in the industrial sector
in the 1980s (Wade 1990, pp. 175 ff.). The essential difference from
the Vietnamese situation, however, is that large private enterprises
played at least an equal role in Korea and Taiwan, the state sector thus
performing an important function, but one that complemented the private sector's.

5.2   Private Enterprises

Before 1988 unified Vietnam had no private enterprises, apart from
family firms, which were politically above suspicion if only because -
officially at least - they did not employ any wage labor. Under the um-
brella of the state-controlled cooperatives, however, there were enterprises run virtually along market-economy lines even at the time of the
planned economy. This was particularly true of the south of the country, where a number of enterprises that had been nationalized in

1975/76 continued to operate under the management of their old owners.

A typical traditional organizational form of small trade and industry that is common, especially in the north of the country, is the industrial village. These villages produce craft products (e.g. furniture, porcelain, silk) under contract. Large trading or industrial enterprises provide raw materials and market the finished products. Not least because these small-scale structures were widespread even at the time of the planned economy and the private sector in the south of the country was suppressed for only about ten years, private trade and industry was able to expand rapidly or to emerge from informality when private enterprise was formally permitted in the late 1980s.

Numerically the most important organizational form of private enterprise is still the family firm in trade, in the service sector and in manufacturing. The number of these enterprises is roughly estimated at between 1 and 1.6 million, with an average of 3 employees each (Wolff et al. 1995, p. 4; Kurths 1997). It was primarily these enterprises that have absorbed the million or so employees made redundant by the state sector, a similar number of demobilized soldiers and the new workers emerging each year owing to population growth (see Table 9).

Most of the industrial cooperatives and quasi-cooperative 'production groups' should also be considered part of this semi-formal private sector. In the past the 50,000 industrial cooperatives were firmly integrated into the planned economy and accounted for some 30 % of industrial production, 50 % of transport operations and 17 % of trade (World Bank 1995a, p. 27). By 1993 only 6,000 industrial cooperatives with about 500,000 employees were left. The others had either gone bankrupt or were being run by members informally as private enterprises. It remains to be seen whether the new 1995 *Cooperatives Law*, which, unlike the rules on the old cooperatives, provides for a clear allocation of property shares to the voluntary members, will lead to the stabilization of the cooperative sector. The continuation of the privatization of the industrial cooperatives is more likely, since the cooperative idea is not deep-rooted in Vietnam, partly because it was used by the state and party as a means of nationalizing property.

While private family firms have to be registered only with the local people's committees, which is inexpensive, the legal entities introduced in 1990/91 - the sole proprietorship, the limited liability company and the joint stock company - must be recorded in the commercial register. For this evidence of minimum capital, which differs from one sector to another, a business plan and various certificates issued by the police, the health authority, a bank (proving adequate financial resources), etc. must be produced. As many businessmen are averse to such expense and, moreover, prefer a semi-formal existence as a family firm to the capitalist forms of enterprise viewed with some skepticism by the party, not many enterprises have yet registered.

Table 11: Registered state-owned and private enterprises		
	1994	1995
Private enterprises	18,497	26,654
- Sole proprietorships	13,532	18,846
- Limited liability companies	5,034	7,635
- Joint stock companies	131	173
State-owned enterprises	6,019	6,446
Source: Ministry of Planning and Investment, Vietnam Investment Review, 20-26 May 1996, p. 1		

Most of the private enterprises are small and medium-sized firms. In 1993 there were only about 500 private enterprises with an invested capital of more than US$ 500,000 (ibid., p. 29), mostly in the food-processing (170), textiles and clothing (97) and wood-processing (50) sectors.

As has already been shown in Table 8, production in the state sector in the first half of the 1990s grew more sharply than in the private sector.

This was partly due to the above-average growth of the state oil and energy sector, although loans were also more freely available and investment was generally higher in the state sector. However, it should be borne in mind that, as the statistics on the private sector are far from complete, it may have developed more dynamically than these figures indicate. This is also the view taken by the government, which is dissatisfied with the results so far achieved with the registration of enterprises. It is assumed that many private enterprises 'hide their capital' and evade taxes, which would explain the still very low tax revenue derived from the private sector (see Table 3). It was therefore announced that all private enterprises would be re-registered in 1996 and that greater pressure would be exerted on large family firms to register in accordance with the legislation on enterprises.[4]

Joint ventures with foreign enterprises are considered to be a separate type of enterprise and not part of the private sector. As most cooperate with state partners, their output is included in the statistics on the state sector. In the next few years, when many joint ventures will be going into operation, this will further stabilize or even increase the state sector's share of GDP.

Table 12: Shares of industrial production, by types of enterprise (%)					
	1989	1990	1991	1992	1993
State-owned enterprises	66,4	67,6	68,5	70,5	71,3
Non-state-owned enterprises	33,6	32,4	31,5	29,5	28,7
- Cooperatives	35,3	28,2	15,3	9,6	8,6
- Private enterprises	3,1	3,0	4,7	9,6	10,8
- Family firms	61,7	68,6	80,0	80,7	80,6
Total	100,0	100,0	100,0	100,0	100,0
Source: World Bank (1995a), p. 32					

Table 12 reveals the change of structure within the non-state sector in industry: while the importance of the cooperatives is rapidly waning, the registered private enterprises' share is growing, without becoming anywhere near as significant as the state-owned enterprises' share. A large, though not accurately quantifiable, proportion of the growth in private enterprises and family firms is due to the takeover of coopera-tives rather than the establishment of new enterprises.

Private enterprises still play a secondary role in foreign trade, as in industrial production. Only about a tenth of the 1,200 export companies are private enterprises. State-owned industrial and trading enterprises dominate in the case of important exports (oil, agricultural products). Recently, however, light industry has been increasing its share of total exports (see Table 6), and as more and more private enterprises obtain export licenses, the private sector's share of foreign trade is likely to grow.

Promotion of the Private Sector

The Vietnamese government's policy towards the private sector is mixed: on the one hand, it is influenced by distrust of capitalist busi-nessmen, the intention being to restrict the growth of their economic power by having a strong state sector, as the 8th Party Congress of the CPV in June 1996 reaffirmed; on the other hand, the government is pursuing a *laissez faire* policy and giving the private sector freedom that is also being exploited by state-owned enterprises to establish pri-vate subsidiaries. Given the state administration's planned-economy background, it understandably sees the promotion of the private sector primarily in terms of control and regulation. Creating the same envi-ronment for all enterprises competing in the market, a basic principle of the market economy, is hardly compatible with the party's concept of a multisectoral economy led by the state, a concept that is influenced by ideology and geared to the retention of power.

There is nonetheless scope for improving the environment for private enterprises without a fundamental political shift of emphasis towards the private sector. Action needs to be taken primarily in four areas: the involvement of bodies representing the private sector in the formulation of policy, the removal of discriminatory regulatory provisions, the improvement of credit supply and access to land use rights.

Dialogue with the private sector: Although independent representative bodies are not in principle permitted in Vietnam, the government has become more willing to accept the existing business associations close to the state as partners in dialogue, although this has so far failed to produce any tangible results in the form of practical improvements. The administration has hitherto been accustomed to direct communication with enterprises. The involvement of bodies representing the business community and of the trade unions in government decision-making processes will require new consultation mechanisms and also competent institutions representing the enterprises.

Three types of association have emerged in recent years:

–   The Vietnam Chamber for Commerce and Industry (*Vietco-chamber/ VCCI*), which in the past was essentially responsible for foreign trade interests and has admitted private enterprises as members only since 1993. By setting up regional chambers - controlled, however, from headquarters - *Vietcochamber* wants to convey the image of being an organization of its members, but will probably concentrate on providing services rather than lobbying, given its traditional dependence on the state and the strong position of state-owned enterprises among its members.

–   The associations of private enterprises which have been established at local and regional level since early 1996 under the supervision of the people's committees after a long political tug-of-war and which see themselves explicitly as the state's interlocutors (Vietnam Investment Review, 21-25 April 1996, p. 5).

–   The Vietnam Union for Cooperatives and Small and Medium Enterprises (VICOOPSME), which emerged from the former association of cooperatives and is looking for new tasks now that many of the cooperatives have collapsed.

None of these bodies has so far been particularly successful in attracting members. They are dependent on government contributions and try to finance their activities by qualifying for development aid resources and running their own enterprises. *Vietcochamber* seems to be emerging as the most important organization, primarily because it is represented throughout the country and the range of services it has to offer is growing.

Eliminating overregulation: Before enterprises may be established or enlarged, extensive authorization procedures must be completed, giving the local people's committees considerable influence on private enterprises. Without an annually renewable license from the authorities, to obtain which the assets of the enterprise, the shareholders' personal circumstances and other details have to be disclosed, no firm may exist as a registered private enterprise. In the expensive and time-consuming examination of applications for the establishment of enterprises and the annual extensions the local planning committees have found a new area of responsibility to replace central planning. In some provinces and municipalities this regulation of the private sector is very much seen as an element of active promotion of the economy. Officials try to protect 'their' enterprises and to help them, for example, to obtain bank loans. Enterprises that do not benefit from this kind of state support tend to find life difficult, especially if they want to expand.

Such authorization procedures have no place in a market-economy system. There must, of course, be means of exercising control over the choice of location for enterprises or their environmental compatibility, for instance, and the financial authorities must have some insight into the financial circumstances of enterprises. These levels of regulation should, however, be dealt with on a separate legal basis. It would then be enough for an enterprise to register once, without any authorization procedures being involved. In particular, the minimum capital requirements and the submission of corporate plans to the authorities as part of the authorization procedure could be abolished immediately.

Another important regulatory instrument used by the state is the allocation of foreign trade licenses. As a minimum turnover is required for the issue of an export license, for example, smaller firms are excluded from exporting direct. The system favors the - now numerous - state-owned firms that handle foreign trade transactions for private enterprises for a commission, which many enterprises consider too high. Few private trading firms have so far been allowed to operate. This procedure in effect amounts to skimming off a rent from export-oriented enterprises, which could be stopped through the abolition of foreign trade licenses and so reduce the transaction costs incurred in exporting.

With a *Law on Domestic Investment* an attempt was made in 1994 to place domestic enterprises on an equal footing in terms of fiscal and other promotional measures with foreign investors benefiting from the *Law on Foreign Investment*. Understandable though this intention was, the outcome has been unsatisfactory. Instead of enshrining some simple promotional measures in legislation, the law provides for sectorally and regionally differentiated tax arrangements, which are linked to the local authorities' authorization procedure and are probably open to negotiation on individual decisions, since the development of a tax authority is still very much in its infancy. A credit fund set up by the law to promote investment is to go into operation in 1996. The original expectation that this fund might primarily benefit private enterprises has not, however, been fulfilled by the government. According to the statements available, it is to be used for state investment in infrastructure.

On the whole, the private enterprises operate in a regulative environment characterized primarily by its unpredictability and the considerable scope it leaves for discretionary decisions by the authorities. Despite a steadily widened legal framework, from the 1990/91 laws on enterprises through the 1992 constitution - which recognized the existence of private enterprises - to the 1995 Civil Code, public action cannot be considered to be bound by the law. For this there is still no administrative law, which would require public decisions to be verifiable.

Improvement of credit supply: As shown in Chapter 4, the availability of loans for the private sector has improved significantly with the reform of the financial sector. However, as the demand for medium- to long-term loans to finance investment cannot be satisfied by any means, most enterprises must resort to their own financial resources, roll over expensive short-term loans (up to 30 % interest p.a.) and tap informal sources of funds. This situation will not change in the foreseeable future, since the main causes of the shortage of long-term capital - the State Bank's stability-oriented interest rate and credit policy, savers' reservations about long-term bank deposits and the difficulty of finding collateral for long-term loans - can be overcome only in the long term. Switching to foreign currency loans at lower interest rates (about 10 % p.a.) is already very popular with state-owned enterprises and large private firms. This might be complemented by long-term concessionary loans from development aid funds, as is already being done in rural financing. The danger with such credit lines, however, is that they tend to discourage the banks from mobilizing local savings capital. In addition, given the present stability of the rate of exchange of the Vietnamese currency, the exchange risk attached to foreign currency loans is generally underrated.

The problems encountered by small and medium-sized firms in finding security for loans could be partly solved if such new instruments as credit guarantee funds were introduced. However, this would require institutional conditions that will take some time to create in Vietnam, through the institutional strengthening of the business associations, for example (Wolff et al. 1995, p. 42).

There is, then, no patent recipe for a rapid improvement in credit supply to private enterprises. Nothing will stand in the way of a gradual increase in the supply of credit if the state restrains its borrowing activities in the capital market, the reorganization of the state-owned commercial banks makes progress and the success achieved with macroeconomic stabilization permits a credit policy that tends to be expansive. A generally beneficial macroeconomic environment, complemented by the consistent strengthening of the institutions in the financial sector, is more important for the private sector than short-term partial solutions, such as the establishment of special credit funds.

Access to land use rights: The Vietnamese constitution defines land as common property which is administered by the state. The 1993 *Land Law* permits the transfer of land use rights acquired from the state and so sanctions, in principle at least, the flourishing grey market in land, which led to speculatively high land prices in the first half of the 1990s, especially in the urban centers. Although private and state-owned enterprises are in principle treated equally in the *Land Law*, the state-owned enterprises are already very well endowed with land, more than they need for actual production in many cases, whereas private enterprises are often able to acquire land use rights only indirectly through state-owned enterprises because of the general shortage of land. The transfer of land use rights is now differentiated in numerous decrees by user and type of land, a different price set by the state applying in each case. This complex system gives rise to a highly segmented land market and difficulties when it comes to using land as collateral for loans (see Chapter 4) and makes it extremely hard for private enterprises to acquire land titles suitable for long-term use. Besides the fees (and taxes) payable to the state for the transfer of land use rights, sums similarly set by the state have to be paid to the previous users in compensation. This is one of the main reasons for foreign investors to secure access to land by entering into a joint venture with a Vietnamese state-owned enterprise.

The need for land to be used efficiently makes it necessary for the prices charged for the transfer of land to be more closely geared to market prices than hitherto. This does not need to infringe the principle of common property: it would be enough to abandon the segmentation of the market, to permit the direct transfer of land without the state's intervention and to limit its influence to the taxation of the transfer and registration in the land register. This would not necessarily make land cheaper for private enterprises, unless the state made land on industrial estates available at reduced prices. Access as such would, however, be far easier, and the security of long-term land titles would enable them to be used as collateral for long-term loans.

5.3   Foreign Direct Investment

Lowering the barriers to foreign direct investment was one of the early fundamental decisions of the Vietnamese reform policy. Although Vietnam was a latecomer with its *Law on Foreign Investment* of December 1987, which was modeled on the investment laws of other countries in the region, it was able to benefit, immediately after opening up to the outside world, from extensive investment by the Asian tiger economies and Japan, which were looking for new locations in the region for labor-intensive production lines. Some 60 % of all investment pledged by the end of 1996 comes from these countries.[5]

The *Law on Foreign Investment* grants tax and import concessions and guarantees the unrestricted transfer of profits. Besides joint ventures, 100 % foreign investment is permitted, though not in all sectors. Increasing advantage is being taken of this opportunity, now that it is apparent that partnership with a state-owned enterprise, the most common model for joint ventures, did not always produce the benefits expected by investors. A particular problem that arose was that, even after the *State Committee for Cooperation and Investment*[6] had given its approval, there remained, particularly at local level, many bureaucratic hurdles which the Vietnamese partner was unable to spare the foreign investor as expected. Added to this, the law requires unanimous decisions by the board of joint ventures even where the Vietnamese partner has a minority holding. In some cases that have been publicized this clause has led to the failure of joint ventures.[7]

Disputes between Vietnamese and foreign partners over the valuation of shares of enterprises occurred in 1995, when the government stipulated in a decree intended to curb land speculation that land was to be valued not at its market value but at the cumulated value of the rent to be paid to the state for a given period. As the Vietnamese partner's contribution to the joint venture usually consists of land, valued at its market value, contracts then had to be renegotiated.

The problems referred to above have helped to make actual investment far slower than expected, and the initial euphoria has now given way to disillusionment, which has been reflected in a sharp decline in commitments since early 1996.[8]

Table 13:	Foreign direct investment, by country of origin[a]		
	Country	Projects	Investment in US$m
1.	Taiwan	273	4,100
2.	Japan	167	2,700
3.	Singapore	148	2,500
4.	Hong Kong	188	2,390
5.	South Korea	174	2,320
6.	USA	63	1,320
7.	Malaysia	51	1,000
8.	France	79	760
9.	Thailand	66	700
10.	British Virgin Islands	38	690
11.	Australia	50	640
12.	Switzerland	17	630
13.	United Kingdom	19	490
14.	Sweden	8	380
15.	Netherlands	26	370
16.	Indonesia	12	330
17.	Bahamas	1	264
18.	Bermuda	7	230
19.	Cayman Islands	5	220
20.	Philippines	11	170
21.	Germany*	13	140
22.	Russia	27	115
	Others	138	414
	Total	1,581	22,873
a authorized projects, at end 1996			
* The scale of German direct investment is somewhat undervalued in the table since some German enterprises, e.g. Daimler-Benz and Triumph, have invested through foreign subsidiaries in Singapore or Liechtenstein			
Source: Ministry of Planning and Investment			

The inflows of foreign direct investment shown in the Vietnamese balance of payments up to and including 1996 total only about 30 % of the investment authorized until that time. Inflows since 1994 have, however, risen sharply, amounting to no less than some 9 - 10 % of GDP in 1995 and so making a major contribution to the increase in the aggregate investment ratio to almost 30 % in 1996 (see Table 4).

Table 14:	Foreign direct investment - commitments and disbursements (US$m)								
	1989	1990	1991	1992	1993	1994	1995	1996	Total
Commit-ments	536	748	1.318	2.290	3.144	3.843	6.328	4.283	22.873
Disburse-ments[a]	100	120	220	260	832	1.048	1.781	2.300	6.661

[a]   Balance-of-payments figures

Source: IMF (1996), p. 258; Ministry of Planning and Investment

Regional Distribution

Foreign direct investment is highly concentrated in geographical terms. While the southern growth triangle around Ho Chi Minh City initially attracted most investment, the north has now caught up somewhat: of the direct investment agreed by the end of 1996, the region around Ho Chi Minh City and the Mekong Delta (Ho Chi Minh City,. Dong Nai, Ba Ria - Vung Tau, Song Be) accounts for about US$ 12 billion and the northern growth triangle around Hanoi and the Red River Delta (Hanoi, Haiphong, Quang Ninh, Hai Hung, Ha Tay, Vinh Phu) for about US$ 7 billion. The remaining 15 % is spread over a further 38 provinces. Nor is this picture likely to change significantly in the medium term, since the agglomeration advantages of the growth triangles - to which the industrial and export zones planned for these regions must be added - easily outweigh the concessions under the *Law on Foreign Investment* for investment in more remote provinces. Only in the central Vietnamese region around Da Nang is the infrastructure such as to permit a greater increase in foreign investment.

Sectoral Distribution

Sectorally, foreign investment in the first few years after the lowering of external barriers focused on the oil and real estate sectors. Largely because of the sharp increase in Japanese and South Korean involvement since 1993, manufacturing now takes first place, accounting for about 50 % of all agreed investment.

Table 15: Foreign direct investment, by sectors[a]		
Sector	Projects	Investment in US$m
Industry	960	11,324
Real estate/hotels	260	7,320
Oil and gas	23	1,187
Transport and telecommuni-cation	51	1,133
Industrial zones	10	624
Agriculture and forestry	51	388
Finance and banking	19	265
Export zones	60	203
Services	72	126
Housing	30	95
Fisheries	23	62
Others	22	143
Total	1,581	22,873

[a]   authorized projects, at end 1996

Source: Ministry of Planning and Investment

The Vietnamese government has recently been trying to exercise more control over the sectoral composition of direct investment. When new investment licenses are allocated, preference is to be given to manufacturing, with the emphasis on technology-intensive and export-oriented investment. There is also demand for investment in infrastructure, especially in the energy sector. In late 1993 a law on the private sponsorship of infrastructure projects (BOT - the *Build-Operate-Transfer* Law) was passed. The legal requirements, particularly regarding the guarantees and collateral instruments needed for long-term project financing, are not yet sufficiently detailed, however. Internal political resistance has so far delayed the progress of the first pilot projects in the infrastructure sphere. The Vietnamese government tends to use not private investment but, for the most part, development aid resources to finance infrastructure projects. It will therefore depend not least on the donors whether pressure is put on Vietnam to finance and operate, say, power stations privately or whether it is permitted to take the easier option of public financing from development aid.

In conjunction with the general disillusionment due to the difficult investment conditions, the attempt to exercise more selective control over foreign investment will probably lead to a decline in new commitments and to the cancellation of projects already agreed. Strikes against poor working conditions in plants established by Korean and Taiwanese investors, together with the new requirement that party cells be established in all foreign enterprises,[9] are also adding to investors uncertainty.

It is quite understandable that the government should try to improve the quality of direct investment. Much of the investment in the first half of the 1990s will tend to be of only short-term benefit to Vietnam. Investment in the real estate and hotel sector exploited excessive price levels in what was initially a very small market, and the invested capital soon paid off. The high profits from such investment led the Vietnamese government to call on the Vietnamese partners to renegotiate and raise the value of the land made available from the usual 30 - 40 % of the equity and so to claim a larger proportion of the profits. Now that supply outstrips demand, the matter has taken care of itself, through the market mechanism. Foreign investors and their (state) Vietnamese partners are now demanding restrictions on market access because prices and profits are falling.

In the textile and clothing sector - another focal area for the first wave of direct investment - the economic benefit to Vietnam is again limited. The production lines that have been installed predominantly by Asian investors, often as 100 % foreign investment, are mostly used for contract processing, with extremely limited value added in Vietnam. The benefit to Vietnam consists in the employment of thousands of young women at a daily wage of about US$ 1, with a modest effect on foreign exchange earnings because so many of the inputs are imported.

The Vietnamese government obviously wants to increase the impact of foreign investment on employment, foreign exchange and especially technology. This will hardly succeed, however, with a negative strategy of discriminating against a few important industries, as reflected in the announcement that applications for investment in the textile and clothing sector will be treated more restrictively in the future (Vietnam Investment Review, 21-26 May 1996, p. 3). More likely to succeed would be a positive strategy of creating an environment conducive to technology-intensive investment and a change from the view that the foreign investor is just a concessionaire who must pay as high a price as possible for exploiting Vietnamese resources to one that sees him as a long-term partner who should be prepared for as comprehensive technology and training transfers as possible and reinvest his profits in Vietnam as far as possible.

Vietnam in Locational Competition

The level and quality of foreign investment in Vietnam are essentially determined by government policies. The country's favorable geographical situation, the domestic market's high growth potential and labor cost advantages make Vietnam a popular investment location in Asia. Whether this potential can be tapped depends on whether the government makes a credible attempt to improve the political and legal environment, particularly for long-term investment. The authorization procedure - shortened from three to two months by the latest amendment of the investment law - plays no more than a secondary role in this context. More important is the clarification of legal and administrative questions relating to the implementation of investment projects: the question of land use rights, the introduction of impartial dispute settlement machinery and the generally more binding nature of public decisions concerning foreign enterprises. The present attitude towards foreign investors is still influenced by a mixture of the Vietnamese partners' desire for quick profits, state authorities' patronage of 'their' joint ventures and widespread corruption due to the wide variety of obscure decision-making channels and a *concept of sovereign immunity* (Scown 1995, p. 31) that provides for individual problems to be settled by negotiation with government institutions rather than by reference to clear administrative regulations. This generally difficult and unpredictable environment compared to other locations in the region is already preventing the absorption of capital not only from the extensive pipeline of projects on which agreement has already been reached but also from international funds seeking suitable investment opportunities (see Chapter 4) and other sources, e.g. for long-term infrastructure project financing.

Although the emerging single ASEAN market is making the region generally more attractive to foreign investors, locational competition within the ASEAN alliance will grow, since one location in the region will be enough for many investors to cover the whole ASEAN market. Vietnam must increase its efforts to attract economically and technologically interesting investment and create appropriate conditions for such investment if it is not eventually to become a second-class, low-wage location in the region. To this end, sectoral strategies must also be developed as the basis for the selective acquisition of investment, so that potential investors may be offered an environment in technologically demanding sectors that is reliable in the long term. This is necessary particularly against the backdrop of the rapidly changing trading environment in the ASEAN context, to which reference was made in Chapter 3. Vietnam must take an interest in achieving an appropriate depth of production in important sectors of manufacturing industry as quickly as possible if it is to stand up to international competition. This will be possible only in cooperation with foreign enterprises, which must be urged and helped to increase the local content of their output as soon as they can. In the automobile sector the Vietnamese government's approach has caused confusion, investment licenses having been issued to a total of 14 foreign enterprises.[10] As the market is still very small (about 40,000 vehicles were sold in 1996), it is doubtful, however, that open competition on this scale will actually persuade the enterprises to effect the high initial investment needed in this sector to achieve a competitive size of plant.

5.4   Prospects for Industrial Development

The reform policy pursued since the late 1980s has greatly improved the environment for the development of the enterprises. The relatively high, two-digit growth rates in the industrial sector (see Table 2), the financial stability of the state-owned enterprises, the flourishing small business sector and the extensive commitments of foreign direct investment cannot, however, conceal the fact that Vietnam's industrial development is still very much in its infancy. Industrial GDP per capita is one of the lowest in Asia; at about US$ 25 per capita, exports of manufactures are at approximately the same level as Bangladesh's.

Despite all the success in stabilizing the economy and employment, the weaknesses of economic transformation are obvious:

–   Although the state enterprise sector is financially stable - management has been quick to learn how to combine market-economy requirements and government protection to the benefit of their enterprises - the Vietnamese government's vision of pressing ahead with the industrialization process while the state-owned enterprises remain largely isolated from international competition seems unrealistic. For this Vietnam lacks both entrepreneurial capacities in the state sector and the financial resources needed for what would tend to be capital-intensive industrialization.

- On the other hand, the development of the private sector, which will always be essential for industrialization that is labor-intensive and thus has a wide impact, is hampered by the dominance of the state sector and a generally unfavorable environment.

- And finally, the tapping of the foreign investment potential for the country's industrialization has so far been hesitant. Ambitious, technology-intensive production lines in the industrial sector and investment in urgently needed infrastructure are in danger of not transpiring because of the unpredictability of the Vietnamese investment climate.

Orientation towards Asian Neighbors

In search of industrial development models Vietnam is naturally being guided by the dynamic newly industrializing countries in the region. What is particularly attractive about these models from the Vietnamese point of view is that in most of these countries politically authoritarian regimes were able, at least in the early stages of their industrialization, to kick-start sustained growth processes with interventionist economic policies. As a model, China too demonstrates, as Vietnam sees it, that there are alternatives to the western economic model in which the state plays a far more dominant role than in liberal market economies.

Beyond this vague orientation towards successful models, there is no clear vision in Vietnam of the process of catch-up industrialization. The major importance attached to the formation of groups of state-owned enterprises and to such strategic investments as oil refineries and steel mills indicates that many of the country's leaders see import substitution as the priority. What is clearly being overlooked in this context is that Vietnam can rely on independent domestic industrialization processes far less than was the case in, say, Korea in the 1960s and 1970s.

This qualification is necessary if only because Vietnam does not rank among the strong developmental states of the Korean, Taiwanese and

Singaporean type. In Vietnam the early reforms in the 1970s and 1980s and the change of system in the 1990s were driven primarily by pressure from the micro level. The strategically and administratively weak state gradually yielded to this pressure, and the further development of the industrial sector is also likely to be determined by the enterprises themselves rather than government targets.

The economic policy decision-makers in Vietnam, unlike the strong states referred to above, are not free from the influence of important lobbies in the business community. Ministries and provincial authorities are often directly dependent on the large state-owned enterprises in their area of jurisdiction. They try to protect them against 'excessive competition' and use their influence with state-owned banks to obtain loans for them. With the growing commercialization of government institutions, the distinction between the state's regulatory function and its role as entrepreneur has become increasingly unclear. As interests are regionally and sectorally fragmented, it is unlikely that coherent industrial policy concepts can be developed against this background. Furthermore, the Vietnamese administration lacks everything that is needed for the fine-tuning of industrial policy measures. There is no group of highly qualified technocrats unswayed by the interests of individual enterprises and therefore no basis for industrial policy interventionism as there was in Korea and Singapore.

Liberal Trade Policy in the ASEAN Context

Furthermore, as the country's borders are open, the Vietnamese government can do little to control the domestic market. This is not only true of consumer goods, which flooded the markets and put heavy pressure on the local consumer goods industry once domestic trade had been liberalized. In recent years there have also been large-scale illegal imports of steel, cement and other construction materials, which the government has been able to do very little to stop if only because some provincial governments and other state institutions were implicated.

Regardless of the de facto openness of the domestic market, the Vietnamese government has committed itself to a liberal foreign trade policy, at least in the regional context, by acceding to ASEAN (see Chapter 3). In the medium term, then, Vietnam will have little scope for import-substituting industries that are not internationally competitive. Given the country's starting position as a latecomer in the regional context, everything indicates that it should exploit its locational advantage in the dynamic East Asian region to the full and from the outset prepare for a regional division of labor that initially casts it in the role of an exporter of labor-intensive manufactures while offering it the prospect, given the size of its domestic market, of developing into the production of primary and intermediate goods. For this Vietnam will be in a better position to take advantage of the greater mobility of international capital than other Asian NICs were able to do in the 1970s and 1980s. In these circumstances there is little room for a pointedly national pattern of industrialization.

Vietnam's starting position thus argues for a relatively open and liberal model of export-oriented industrialization with a strong private sector that seizes all the many opportunities for linkages with private enterprises in the region, such as the Chinese foreign trade networks.

Promotion of Small and Medium-sized Private Enterprises

The strengthening of the private sector should begin primarily with medium-sized enterprises that are potentially capable of adapting modern technologies and producing for export. It is here, i.e. with some of the 26,800 registered private enterprises (see Table 11), that the greatest constraint on, but also the greatest potential for, Vietnamese industrial development exists. The environment, and above all access to credit and commercial premises, needs to be appreciably improved for manufacturing enterprises with 50 or more employees. The technological upgrading of these firms could be promoted by government assistance through the many state and parastatal R&D institutions, which are under heavy pressure to commercialize. Like some state-owned enterprises, they have qualified technical personnel who have not yet been adequately used for the private sector.[11]

Given the political distrust of capitalist enterprises and the shortage of qualified administrative capacities, it is unlikely that such initiatives will be taken by government. The World Bank/ IFC and the European Union have recently been putting together a sizeable consultancy and financial package (*project development facility*) in an attempt to make the investment projects of medium-sized private enterprises eligible for bank loans and so to promote the expansion of the private sector. This might also help to involve private firms more heavily in international cooperation between enterprises than in the past and make them interesting partners for foreign investors.

The example of the highly dynamic *township and village enterprises*, which made major contributions to the development of employment and exports in China in the space of a few years, cannot, however, be imitated in Vietnam. Although there is a symbiosis of government administration with local enterprises at local level that is certainly comparable with the Chinese situation, some of the requirements that helped this model to succeed in China are not satisfied in Vietnam: the longer tradition of rural industrialization since the 1960s, with the not insignificant development of human resources and technological capacities, the availability of capital at local level and the protection of consumer goods production by state-administered prices in the start-up phase. In contrast, rural industrialization in Vietnam has only just begun and will not be able to achieve the same dynamism as in China. This makes it all the more important for the potential of the - predominantly urban - private sector to be consistently promoted, since the desired export-oriented industrial dynamism will not otherwise be achieved.

6 Environment, Industrialization and Sustainable Development

6.1 Fragile Natural Foundations of the Development Process

In most of the dynamic developing countries of the South-East Asian region it was not until the 1980s that the ecological implications of rapid growth were recognized and the first policy adjustments were initiated to introduce sustainable development processes. These countries had previously spent several decades building up their capital stock without regard for the ecological costs, the rising consumption of natural resources or the adverse implications for the people's quality of life. They pursued a strategy of 'polluting now and paying later', which is now proving very expensive - in terms of repairing environmental damage in the urban agglomerations, for example.

For Vietnam this strategy is not a realistic option. For one thing, damage to the environment is already well advanced despite the many years of economic stagnation. For another, the country's resource base related to population is far narrower than was the case in other South-East Asian countries when they began their dynamic development process. Despite not inconsiderable oil, coal and iron ore reserves and an agricultural potential still capable of expansion, Vietnam is unable to resort to the natural-resource based export orientation adopted by Indonesia and Malaysia in the 1960s and 1970s, since high domestic consumption limits exportable surpluses and there are no reserves of land for extensive agriculture. This limitation of natural resources alone forces Vietnam to adopt a strategy of intensive and yet eco-friendly development of agriculture, manufacturing industry and the service sector.

This puts Vietnam at a disadvantage compared to other South-East Asian countries. It cannot go through the usual development sequences and begin to reduce its consumption of natural resources only when it achieves newly industrializing country status. Taking account of environmental costs will thus make the Vietnamese development process more expensive than that of the South-East Asian NICs. On the other hand, the principle that preventive measures, and especially the use of eco-efficient technologies, are far cheaper than the later repair of environmental damage is particularly true of industrial pollution. International experience shows that a substantial proportion of industrial pollution can be avoided at a relatively minor increase in capital and production costs (World Bank 1992, pp. 126 ff.). By using the latest technologies that have already been tried out in industrialized countries, Vietnam thus has an opportunity to gain cost advantages over other countries which are having to resort to costly investment to repair the environmental damage done by old technologies.

For Vietnam this means incorporating the objectives and instruments associated with the concept of sustainable development in its transformation and development policies from the outset, not only to avoid long-term damage but especially because of the fragile natural base from which the Vietnamese modernization process is being launched.

Shortage of Land and Population Pressure

At 210 inhabitants per square kilometer, Vietnam's average population density is similar to Thailand's and the Philippines'. However, as only 21 % of the area of the country is used for agriculture and 73 % of the workforce is employed in agriculture, the utilized agricultural area per employee is one of the smallest in the world: it averages 0.13 ha and, in the Red River Delta in northern Vietnam, as little as 0.06 ha (World Bank 1995b, p. 6).

The shortage of land is further exacerbated by the fact that the soil outside the river deltas is largely of medium to poor quality. An added factor is the continuing erosion due primarily to the deforestation and inappropriate cultivation of slopes, the sedimentation of reservoirs and irrigation systems and the salination of soils in parts of the river deltas (Reed 1996, pp. 270 f.).

Vietnam's population (about 72 million in 1995) is growing at 2.1 % p.a., the birth rate in the rural areas being about twice as high as in the towns and cities. The population pressure is particularly pronounced in the mountainous regions, which are home to the ethnic minorities that make up about 17 % of Vietnam's population.

Deforestation

Since the mid-1940s Vietnam's forested area has shrunk from 67 to 29 %. The annual deforestation rate is currently about 2 % (ibid., p. 272). The greatest loss of forest land has occurred in the northern mountainous regions, where it has dwindled from 95 to 17 % in the past 50 years.

The causes of deforestation are varied and differ from one region to another. In northern and central Vietnam the expansion of agricultural land was the most important factor. Forests are also used as sources of firewood and for the legal and illegal commercial logging: since the ban on exports of round timber imposed in 1991 it has been permitted only to meet the domestic requirements of the paper and furniture industries. The effects of the war play no more than a secondary role in this context. Although extensive damage was done to the forests by the bombing and defoliation of large areas from 1965 to 1973, its long-term impact pales into insignificance when compared to the effects of the permanent expansion of agricultural land and long-term overutilization of the forests (World Bank 1995b, Annex 4).

Deforestation has led to large areas that can no longer be farmed, to erosion and sedimentation and to increasing damage due to flooding in the plains. The World Bank puts the income lost because of erosion in just one area of some 2.5 million hectares in northern Vietnam (Da watershed) at US$ 140 million, thus providing an economic justification for reafforestation measures (World Bank 1995b, pp. 254 ff.).

Besides the inland forested areas, the mangrove forests on the coast and in the river deltas are at serious risk. Inappropriate methods of aquaculture, especially shrimp farming, are causing a permanent loss of quality in valuable wetlands, resulting in declining yields.

Industrial Pollution

Compared to other South-East Asian countries, Vietnam's industrial sector is modest in size. Its share of GNP is 23 % as against about 39 % in both Thailand and Indonesia. Industrial output is about one tenth of Thailand's. It is, however, perfectly realistic to assume that the industrial sector will continue to grow at two-digit annual rates in the long term, as it did in the first half of the 1990s, and that the number of industrial enterprises will therefore multiply.

At present environmental problems are occurring essentially at the locations of large enterprises engaged in heavy industry, e.g. cement, fertilizer and paper production, coal mining and power generation. These enterprises are located predominantly in the two growth triangles of Hanoi / Haiphong / Quang Ninh and Ho Chi Minh City / Bien Hoa / Vung Tau. The problems of industrial pollution will continue to focus on these industrial centers in the future, since increasing agglomeration there can hardly be avoided despite incentives for regionally decentralized industrial development. This also means that the growth triangles, including the planned third triangle around Da Nang in central Vietnam, will be exposed to an urbanization process familiar from other Asian mega cities.

The urban centers already face serious water and air quality problems. Sewerage systems - where they exist - are in a poor state. Domestic and industrial effluent is discharged into the rivers untreated, the proportion of industrial effluent steadily growing. This is already having a noticeable impact on public health (World Bank 1995a, pp. 161 f.). The increasing competition between urban, industrial and agricultural consumers of natural resources, especially land and water, is also making itself felt, however.

6.2   State Environmental Policy

The effects of the policy of economic reform on the environment have so far been mixed. The introduction of market mechanisms, and especially the price reform, paved the way for more efficient resource use. The liberalization of foreign trade and the lowering of the barriers to foreign direct investment has led to orientation towards labor-intensive production lines in light industry that do less damage to the environment than heavy industry. The "clean" service sector is expanding. As a rule, the imported technologies are far more eco-efficient than the existing obsolete capital stock.

On the other hand, high growth rates continue to pose a threat to the environment. The tariffs charged for such important resources as water and energy do not cover costs, largely because capital costs are undervalued in the calculation of these tariffs. The ownership of land and forests is often not clearly defined, and there are no regulatory mechanisms for internalizing the cost of consuming natural resources. In some sectors, e.g. aquaculture, this is resulting in the rapid degradation of the basic means of production. As its resource base is narrow and population pressure is high, Vietnam therefore runs a serious risk of soon feeling the effects of reaching the limits to unbridled growth, unless it adjusts its environmental policy.

Important legal and institutional foundations for the incorporation of ecological aspects in the economic and development policies have been laid since the early 1990s:

–   In 1991 the government came forward with the first *National Plan for Environmentally Sustainable Development*. The plan was the outcome of a debate on the environment prompted by Vietnamese scientists in the 1980s, which was also well received in the Communist Party - with reference, among other things, to Ho Chi Minh's early reafforestation programs - and was subsequently supported by international NGOs (IUCN, WWF) (Jamison and Baark 1995, pp. 277 f.).

– In 1993 the parliament passed an *Environmental Protection Law*, which defines the institutional division of labor and provides for the introduction of environmental policy instruments (e.g. environmental impact assessment for large projects).

– In 1995 the Ministry of Planning and Investment submitted a *Sustainable Development Plan* for the period 1996 - 2010, which incorporates a National Environmental Action Plan. The plan announces a change of strategy from the repair of environmental damage (e.g. reafforestation) to the prevention and control of developments harmful to the environment. In the medium term public spending on this is to be raised from the present 0.3 % of GNP to 1 %, which is equivalent to the average in other South-East Asian countries (World Bank 1995a, p. 152).

The main institutions responsible for implementing the above are the Ministry of Science, Technology and the Environment (MOSTE), which emerged from the State Science Commission in 1992, the National Environment Agency, which was established in 1993 and comes under the MOSTE, and the Ministry of Planning and Investment, which is responsible both for long-term development planning and for the control and authorization of domestic and foreign investment. The two ministries are represented at provincial level by appropriate divisions attached to the people's committees, although it would appear that only in Hanoi and Ho Chi Minh City has it so far proved possible to set up environmental divisions capable of performing the functions expected of them.

Implementation Problems

With this legal and institutional framework, initial foundations have been laid for the integration of ecological aspects into the economic and development policies, but the implementation of policy at working level is still encountering major obstacles. Thus the terms of reference of the institutions responsible are not clearly defined; there is no machinery for settling disputes between the planning and environment ministries or between central and provincial authorities. Furthermore, the sectoral ministries responsible for important state-owned enterprises still carry considerable weight in decision-making on investment, locations and technologies. Even more important is that, as the institutions lack qualified personnel and a clear mandate, they are currently able to cope with only a few high-priority tasks, such as environmental impact assessments of large projects and the case-by-case inspection of plants following complaints about damage to the environment.[1]

The expansion of institutional capacities and the definition of their tasks with regard, say, to the adoption of environmental standards and procedures for ensuring compliance with them need to be accomplished in the immediate future, an area in which international cooperation can also make major contributions. There are still no procedures for involving the public or groups directly concerned in important decisions with ecological implications - and they are hardly conceivable in the present political context. As many projects in Vietnam depend on international financial contributions, appropriate conditionality may improve participation and transparency in decision-making. The World Bank points out, for example, that "... international lending agencies like the World Bank will not finance projects which require an environmental assessment unless there has been adequate public participation." (World Bank 1995b, p. 113)

Industrial Pollution

Probably the most difficult environmental tasks for the Vietnamese government are related to industrialization and the urbanization associated with it. In industrial strategy terms orientation towards the goal of ecological sustainability means specialization in clean industries whose consumption of natural resources is low, the use of best practice technologies by domestic and foreign investors and the avoidance of the wastage of natural resources and pollution in natural-resource-intensive industries.

To this end, the political and institutional framework referred to above must undergo further development and be implemented at micro level in the next few years:

– The legal framework must be defined through the adoption of suitable standards and the development of monitoring and enforcement instruments.

– Management capacities at central and local level must be improved through extensive training schemes, for example.

– The environmental policy *command and control* instruments that take the forefront in the logic of an administration influenced by a planned economy must be complemented by market-economy instruments geared to the internalization of environmental costs and to the polluter-pays principle.

– The choice of locations by industrial enterprises must be controlled by regional and urban development plans and by the planning of industrial estates with appropriate infrastructure.

– The procedure for the environmental impact assessment of new industrial projects must be defined and applied to the state and private sectors alike.

– To prevent damage to the environment, specific programs must be developed for individual industrial subsectors (e.g. food-processing, chemical industry), with the enterprises involved in this process.

As the institutional capacities are limited, it is doubtful that this ambitious agenda, which is set out here only for the industrial sector as an example, can be implemented within an appropriate time frame. The administration will come close to satisfactorily performing the tasks outlined only if it has the support of international contributions and initiatives taken by the business community itself.

There is considerable willingness among international donors to assist environmental projects; as elsewhere, however, donor coordination leaves something to be desired. As the agenda outlined for the industrial sector shows, financial contributions are less important than the formulation of policies and the development of institutional capacities. If the Vietnamese authorities have the political will, it should not be all too difficult to design a medium-term program for institution-building with foreign assistance based on a division of labor among donors.

The business community itself, and especially the foreign enterprises, are urged, in their own long-term interests, to play an active role in environmental policy, to market environmentally friendly products and technologies and to apply the OECD countries' standards to their product lines in Vietnam. Only then can Vietnam succeed in avoiding the costly detour through the "dark satanic mills phase of industrial growth" (World Bank 1992, p. 127).

7   Poverty Alleviation, Rural Development and Social Policy

7.1   Vietnam's Poverty Profile

The average annual per capita income in Vietnam of about US$ 200 is an indication of widespread poverty. However, this average figure conceals major differences in personal and regional income distribution that are not recorded statistically, but are needed if the scale and distribution of absolute poverty are to be determined.

Some initial information on Vietnam's poverty profile is provided by a representative survey of 4,800 households that was carried out in towns and rural communities of Vietnam's seven main regions in 1992 and 1993.[1] Table 17 gives an overview of the most important findings of this survey.

At the time of the survey 51 % of the Vietnamese population could be classified as absolutely poor, i.e. their expenditure on food and non-food amounted to less than that needed for a minimum basket determined by internationally comparable standards (poverty line). Despite all the qualifications regarding the international comparability of such highly aggregated figures, the comparison with other Asian countries - China (9 %), Indonesia (15 %), the Philippines (21 %), Thailand (16 %) - shows how far behind Vietnam is lagging. The proportion of the absolutely poor in the South-East Asian countries two to three decades ago was, however, just as high as it is in Vietnam today.

Table 16:	Incidence of poverty and per capita expenditure on consumption, by regions					
Region	Rural		Urban		Total	
	%[a]	1,000 dong[b]	%[a]	1,000 dong[b]	%[a]	1,000 dong[b]
North Mountains	63	936	34	1,415	59	1,007
Red River Delta	55	1,151	15	2,457	49	1,340
North Coast	74	934	42	1,401	71	974
Central Coast	54	1,239	36	1,951	49	1,457
Central Highlands	50	1,159	-	-	50	1,159
South East	45	1,610	17	2,509	33	2,008
Mekong Delta	52	1,300	28	2,453	48	1,506
Weighted average	57	1,189	26	1,741	51	1,373 (US$ 129)

[a] Percentage of the population below the poverty line. The poverty line is defined as a household's expenditure on consumption equivalent to the consumption of 2,100 calories per capita and day and an additional amount for non-food. Regional price differences result in regionally different poverty lines.

[b] Real annual expenditure on consumption per capita; 1992 prices

Source: World Bank (1995c)

The regional differences are very pronounced, as are the differences between urban and rural areas. The northern coastal and mountainous regions have the highest proportion of absolutely poor people, the urban regions of Hanoi (Red River Delta, urban) and Ho Chi Minh City (South-East, urban) the lowest proportion, per capita expenditure on consumption in the latter being two and a half times higher than in the poorest regions. That 52 % of the rural population of the Mekong Delta, which is regarded as relatively wealthy, are counted among the absolutely poor goes to show that poverty is most heavily concentrated in the rural areas, where 80 % of the population live.

The high incidence of poverty corresponds to a relatively 'equal' income distribution: Vietnam's Gini coefficient is, at 36 %, the same as China's and well below those of such other South-East Asian countries as Thailand (43 %) and the Philippines (41 %) (World Bank 1994, p. 82). The extremely low level of consumption by a large proportion of the population contrasts, however, with relatively favorable indicators in the education and health sectors, where Vietnam differs sharply from other poor developing countries: the literacy rate, for example, is 88 %, average life expectancy 67 years. Infant mortality is a third of the average in the poorest developing countries. However, the low level of consumption among the absolutely poor is also reflected in a high rate of malnutrition and disturbances of growth in almost half of all children under the age of five (ibid).

The available data do not yet allow of any statements on changes in the poverty situation since the beginning of the reform policy. It is interesting to note, however, that in a survey of 120 rural communities conducted at the same time as the household survey, in 114 communities a subjective impression conveyed was that the quality of life had changed for the better in the past five years, the main cause being seen as the change of agricultural policy (decollectivization, liberalization of prices) (World Bank 1995c, p. 9). It is clear from this finding that the rural population benefited from the liberalization measures in the first phase of the reform. Absolute poverty in rural areas had obviously been far more common before the reform. To reduce the incidence of poverty further, structural rural development measures will be very important, since the scope for liberalization measures in this sphere has been largely exhausted.

The high incidence of poverty in rural areas indicates the need for the emphasis to be placed on rural development. However, a political dilemma then arises for the Vietnamese government: if it is assumed that investment in rural areas and agriculture will increase productivity less than investment in the urban 'growth triangles' and industry, a trade-off occurs between macroeconomic growth and rural development. Diverting public investment and credit flows into rural areas may result in a reduction of macroeconomic growth. As, however, rural development must be seen not only in terms of reducing poverty but also as a requirement for reducing migration to the towns and cities and as a basis for the development of domestic economic linkages, everything argues, from the long-term economic angle, for increased promotion of investment in the rural areas.

There are many indications that regional and social inequality has worsened since the beginning of the economic reforms, principally because of the rapid economic upswing in Ho Chi Minh City and Hanoi. It is precisely because private capital flows to the centers are high (see section 5.3 for the regional concentration of foreign direct investment) that it is absolutely essential for state transfers to perform a compensatory function for infrastructure and social services in the rural areas.

7.2   Rural Development

In view of the very different climatic and geographical conditions in various parts of the country the requirements for rural development processes vary widely. The different historical processes in northern and southern Vietnam also help to make the starting conditions in the two parts of the country different: the somewhat less equal distribution of land, the greater availability of capital thanks to remittances from expatriate Vietnamese and the greater entrepreneurial experience favor the modernization of agriculture in the south. The north, on the other hand, has traditionally had better social services, especially in the health and education sectors. The very small utilized agricultural area per household makes it difficult, however, to convert productivity increases into higher family incomes.

The different starting conditions give rise to different points of departure for rural development programs. However, they all seek

–   to increase agricultural productivity by improving methods of cultivation, the supply of inputs and the diversification of production;

–   to develop non-agricultural sources of income, for which an increase in agricultural yields is, however, often the most important requirement, since in the poorest rural areas in particular effective demand for non-agricultural goods and services is not being generated.

From the wide range of instruments for promoting rural development two areas that seem especially important will be singled out here: the development of a market in agricultural land and the improvement of rural infrastructure. A third key factor in rural development, the improvement of the supply of credit, has already been considered in Chapter 4.

In the north of the country in particular the process of collectivizing agriculture and the allocation of individual plots after the dissolution of the production cooperatives in the late 1980s resulted in very small agricultural plots, which produce relatively high yields - the rice monoculture in the Red River Delta being an example - but are hardly suitable as an economic basis for substantial improvements in income, given their small size and the rise in population pressure. As most of the population has hitherto been entirely dependent on agriculture for incomes, population growth has led to increasing rural underemployment, which can be countered only with migration to flourishing urban areas or a growing supply of non-agricultural employment opportunities.

Under its 1994 plan for renewing the structure of the rural economy the government intends, for example, to increase the proportion of non-agricultural employment in the Red River Delta from about 12 % in 1994 to about 30 % in the year 2000 (UNDP 1995, p. 5). This target can be achieved only if the amalgamation of plots and diversification away from the rice monoculture lead to a rapid increase in agricultural incomes and so in demand for consumer goods, services and agricultural inputs. This in turn presupposes that some of the population are prepared to sell or let plots that are too small and farmed unproductively and to look for employment outside agriculture.

Although the 1993 *Land Law* paved the way for the transfer of land use rights, the market in agricultural land still takes the form of a grey area of informal arrangements, since some use rights have not been entirely clarified and the rules and procedures relating to letting and the rules on the settlement of disputes and rival claims lack transparency. Until land titles themselves and the conditions governing their transfer are clear, there will be difficulties not only with the productivity-oriented reallocation of agricultural land but also with the use of land as collateral for long-term loans (see Chapter 4).

The question of the distribution of agricultural land is clearly a highly explosive issue in political and social terms. Unless the supply of jobs in rural trade and industry increases rapidly, the number of landless peasants and the danger of massive migratory movements to the urban areas will grow. Now that the state has largely withdrawn from the agricultural sector, however, further structural change can hardly be curbed. A clear legal framework would probably give the state stronger indirect regulatory options - through the tax system, for example - than is the case under the present strategy, which leaves land distribution to the grey market.

The improvement of rural infrastructure, another key factor, is very important not only for increasing the productivity of agriculture itself but also for the development of non-agricultural trade and industry. The findings of the 1992/93 *Living Standard Survey* show that average expenditure on consumption in communities with access to an asphalt road is significantly higher than in communities without a road of this kind (World Bank 1995c, p. 16). Better communications improve the chances of marketing agricultural products and the prospects of alternative employment opportunities. The data show that these factors correlate positively with a higher standard of living (ibid.).

After decades of extremely low public investment in infrastructure such other sectors as energy and water supply are also in a desolate state. The government is concentrating its efforts on rehabilitating and expanding large supraregional infrastructure projects. The budgets of the provinces, districts and municipalities cover only some of the necessary maintenance costs. For investment in infrastructure at local level the system of interregional financial relations would have to be modified to enable the provinces and municipalities to meet at least some local requirements from their own resources. The prospects for policies that reduce poverty in rural areas are closely linked to the question of local financial autonomy and the decentralization of planning and de-cision-making processes.

7.3 Interregional Financial Relations and Decentralization

The change in the financing of the national budget from state-owned enterprises' transfers to taxes as the state's main source of revenue resulted - on paper at least - in the centralization of interregional fi-nancial relations. In principle, central government has since been enti-tled to all tax revenue and allocates some of it to the provinces. In 1992, for example, about 35 % of state expenditure was based on fi-nancial allocations from central government to the provincial govern-ments (Bird, Litvack and Rao 1995, p. 9). In this way the provinces finance smaller regional and local investment projects (about 15 % of expenditure) and are responsible for their maintenance and for recur-rent costs (about 85 %).

In practice, however, the system of financial relations is less central-ized, largely because the tax system is still being developed and accu-rate planning of financial flows is difficult since tax revenues fluctuate wildly and are not easy to predict.

The level and composition of the provincial budgets are thus deter-mined in a process of negotiation between the provincial and central governments on the basis of estimated tax revenue and approved by the parliament together with the national budget. On the basis of this ex-penditure ceiling some of the taxes collected by the local tax authori-ties are allocated to the provinces. If tax revenue is higher than pre-dicted - a regular occurrence in recent years, in the flourishing prov-inces at least - fresh negotiations are held on its distribution. The province's share of the tax revenue of the following year will be lower, however. If the revenue is lower than predicted, negotiations are held on additional allocations by central government. The disadvantage of this system is that the rich provinces with revenue higher than estimated find themselves in a privileged position compared to the poor provinces. Their expenditure per capita of the population is accordingly significantly higher than in the poor provinces (ibid., p. 23). Furthermore, the system is unpredictable because the provinces' shares of the tax revenue have to be determined anew each year and leaves the provinces little autonomy in determining their expenditure and little incentive to mobilize funds of their own.

From the angle of poverty alleviation, however, it is not only the discrimination against the poor provinces with their disproportionately large share of the absolutely poor that must be criticized but also the generally extremely small amount that can be spent at local level on poverty-oriented investment in economic and social infrastructure. In 1992 the funds available per capita at provincial level averaged about US$ 12, of which about US$ 2 could be used for investment (ibid., p. 10). On so narrow a financial base only a minimum supply level can be maintained. The provinces' attempts to improve their bargaining position in the budget negotiations with central government by submitting numerous investment applications are, as a rule, doomed to failure, central government's decisions on the investment to be effected usually lacking transparency. This system is thus very similar to the negotiating processes that formed part of central economic planning.

In addition to their share of the tax revenue the provinces receive tied allocations from central government programs, among them a poverty alleviation and a job creation program, although the sums concerned are so small that they can have no significant impact.

The provision made in the present system for the financing of the municipalities is very inadequate. They receive financial allocations from the provinces, but are usually so poorly endowed with funds that important investment in maintenance can be effected only if the local people volunteer their labor.

Precisely because of the high economic growth and - therefore - high tax revenue it would be appropriate for a larger proportion of state expenditure to be switched to regional and local level. Gearing expenditure more closely to the local need for investment in economic and social infrastructure and greater transparency of decision-making processes at local level argue for fiscal decentralization in accordance with the subsidiarity principle. Greater financial autonomy might also be reflected in the assignment to the municipalities and provinces of limited power to levy taxes. Financial allocations from central government should be geared more closely to regional equalization and guaranteeing a minimum financial endowment for poor provinces than has been the case in the past. Tied financial allocations might be linked to the mobilization of local funds.

The new *Budget Law* passed in 1996 includes the beginnings of greater fiscal decentralization. A question that remains largely unanswered, however, is how to finance the municipalities, which could play a particularly important role in the provision of basic social services and infrastructure.

7.4   Social Policy

The reform of the economy has given rise to sweeping changes in the organization and financing of the education and health systems and of the social safety nets. While the state-owned enterprises and cooperatives once provided for a large proportion of the social services, a new institutional basis now has to be found for them. Although recurrent state spending on education and health rose when the reform of the economy began, as Table 17 shows, its share of GDP is far smaller than in comparable Asian countries. The largest proportion of the state social budget is, moreover, used to pay for the pensions of civil servants and war veterans, i.e. it does not benefit the poorest sections of the population.

Table 17:	The social sectors' share of recurrent state spending (% of GDP)								
	1986	1987	1988	1989	1990	1991	1992	1993	1994
General administration	0.9	0.7	0.9	1.6	1.6	1.7	2.3	2.4	2.3
Administration of the economy	3.3	2.0	1.0	1.4	1.2	1.0	1.3	2.2	1.9
Social expenditure	3.2	2.5	2.2	4.5	4.8	4.4	5.6	7.9	8.0
- Education	1.3	1.1	0.6	1.1	1.0	1.0	1.4	2.1	2.2
- Health	0.5	0.5	0.5	0.7	0.9	0.8	1.0	1.2	1.1
Other	6.3	8.5	9.8	7.9	7.1	4.3	4.8	6.3	6.1
Total recurrent expenditure (excluding interest)	13.7	13.7	13.9	15.4	14.7	11.4	14.0	18.8	18.3
Source: World Bank (1995a)									

In spending on education and health too there is evidence of a clear bias towards the urban areas and higher income brackets (World Bank 1995c, pp. 82 ff.). This is a threat to Vietnam's relatively favorable social indicators, especially its high literacy rate. Initial signs of a deterioration of the social system are falling school enrollment rates and a decline in the use of health services. This is essentially due to the fees that all users have been charged since the late 1980s. To prevent any further erosion of the rural education and health systems in particular, the government will have to invest more in basic facilities - primary schools and primary health care - so that the fees for these services may be reduced or at least differentiated according to means. A significant proportion of secondary and tertiary education and high-quality health services will probably have to continue being financed privately. As in other Asian countries, at least some of the people are prepared to invest a relatively large proportion of their income in education.

The social security system, 90 % of which benefits former civil servants and war veterans, so burdens the budget that little scope is left for transfers specifically to poor sections of the population. A possible solution would be to transfer pension payments to a separate social insurance system increasingly financed from contributions. While in the past only state-owned enterprises were required to pay 15 % of their total wage and salary bill as their social insurance contribution (10 % to the Finance Ministry, 5 % to the trade unions, which perform the tasks of an accident insurance fund), private enterprises have also been included in this scheme since 1993. As the state-owned enterprises have contributed only about a third of what is required of them in recent years, there has been a considerable need for subsidization, which has had to come from the budget.

7.5   Prospects for Poverty Alleviation

As growth rates have been high in recent years, the number of the absolutely poor - calculated by reference to the poverty line defined in the 1992/93 *Living Standard Survey* - has in all probability already fallen significantly. The World Bank estimates that at an average annual growth rate of 8 % - with differences between regional growth rates and income distribution unchanged - the proportion of the absolutely poor can be reduced from 51 to 29 % of the population by the year 2000 (ibid., p. 27). Assuming that income distribution tends to deteriorate as development continues, the achievement of this objective will depend primarily on the deliberate reallocation of resources to the rural areas and on the reorientation of the social policy to benefit the poor. Currently, there are many indications that the government is entirely focused on the process of industrial modernization in the centers and continuing to neglect the rural areas.

Labor-intensive and export-oriented investment will probably create many jobs in manufacturing industry in the future and rapidly reduce urban poverty. Uncontrolled migration from rural areas would give rise to fresh social and ecological costs which would again burden public budgets at the expense of poorer regions. Everything therefore argues for the Vietnamese government making a massive effort to improve the rural infrastructure and credit system, even at the expense of somewhat lower growth rates in the centers. In view of the economic dynamism that exists, indirect productivity-promoting policies, if implemented consistently, are likely, moreover, to have a greater poverty-reducing impact than socially oriented transfers, such as the Vietnamese Employment Ministry's highly subsidized credit programs for poverty alleviation and job creation, which merely distract attention from the real structural policy tasks.

8   The Role of Development Cooperation

8.1   Transformation without Outside Help

Vietnam has always been dependent on foreign aid. While the country was divided and during the second Indochina war, it received extensive economic aid from the protecting powers - the USA on the one hand and the Soviet Union and China on the other (see Chapter 2). Once the country was unified, it was primarily the member countries of the CMEA that made major contributions to the development of (heavy) industry and large state farms and in the infrastructure sphere. It is difficult to determine the scale of CMEA aid because it took the form of a complex web of trade, supply and credit agreements that was not based on world market prices. A typical example would be the linking of the supply of equipment to the export of raw materials (coffee, rubber, pepper) or simple consumer goods, or the partial redemption of credit obligations through the export of labor. In some years such aid is said to have amounted to about US$ 1 billion, or roughly 10 % of Vietnam's national product.

After the end of the war there were also many humanitarian aid projects from various sources and a number of rehabilitation projects financed by western and multilateral donors, including the World Bank. The only western donors to continue providing development aid on any appreciable scale after Vietnam's invasion of Cambodia in 1979 were the Scandinavian countries, foremost among them Sweden, which financed, for example, the construction of a state paper mill, a large project that proved to be a bottomless pit and tended in retrospect to be an object of Swedish (self-)criticism.

After the collapse of the Soviet Union, the GDR and the CMEA no more foreign aid of any note was available for Vietnam. The prospect of a decline in economic aid from the CMEA, of which there had been signs since 1987 (see note 3, Chapter 3), may have helped to accelerate the reform process. In having no external aid of any kind to cushion the sweeping structural changes to the economy in the difficult years of 1990 to 1992, however, Vietnam differs from other transforming countries that were able at an early stage to take advantage of aid provided, in particular, by the international financial institutions. It is all the more remarkable that the decisive steps in the reform were taken at this of all times and that the macroeconomic situation, the still relatively high rate of inflation aside, remained largely stable.

It was primarily the achievements at this time which gained Vietnam the international reputation of being particularly reform-oriented and therefore deserving of support. While the multilateral financial institutions were still being restrained by the USA's veto, some bilateral donors - among them the Federal Republic of Germany - began to prepare for development cooperation with Vietnam in 1990/91 (Radke and Wolff 1990). However, provision was initially made only for technical cooperation, financial allocations still being blocked by Vietnam's unsettled debts - to the IMF among others. It was primarily on France's and Japan's initiative that both the problem of the IMF debt and the USA's opposition to any support for Vietnam from the international financial institutions were overcome. Consequently, bilateral and multilateral development cooperation with Vietnam gradually began to take shape in 1991/92, although it took some time for disbursements to occur on any appreciable scale.

8.2   Consultative Group for Vietnam

Since 1993 the *Consultative Group for Vietnam* has been the main forum for the coordination of development cooperation with Vietnam. Under the chairmanship of the World Bank some 20 bilateral donors, all the relevant multilateral donors and the Vietnamese government, represented by the Deputy Prime Minister, meet annually - usually in Paris, but in Hanoi in 1996 - to discuss Vietnam's development policy and the scale of international aid.

The *Consultative Group's* coordinating function is, however, of a global nature and does not concern the donors' individual efforts. The coordination of projects and programs is essentially Vietnam's responsibility, its Ministry of Planning and Investment playing the principal steering role.

Table 18: Development aid under the auspices of the *Consultative Group for Vietnam* (US$m)		
	Commitments	Disbursements
1993	1,860	287
1994	2,000	607
1995	2,300	430
1996	2,400	663
Sources: IMF, BMZ		

At the *Consultative Group*'s first four meetings a total of some US$ 8.5 billion of official development assistance (ODA) was committed in the form of grants or loans (with a grant element of at least 25 %). The majority of this (about 70 %) consisted of financial commitments to investment in economic and social infrastructure. The remainder is available for balance-of-payments loans (to finance imports) and for technical cooperation measures.

With commitments of more than US$ 3 billion (1993-96), Japan is by far the largest donor. The vast majority of Japanese aid consists of low-interest yen loans for infrastructure projects, mostly in the energy and transport sectors. It is followed by the World Bank, with about US$ 1.8 billion, and the Asian Development Bank, with about US$ 1 billion. Together, these three donors account for about two thirds of development aid to Vietnam.

While the first technical cooperation projects, primarily in the training and economic consultancy spheres, began in 1991/92, the disbursement of financial cooperation grants and loans were slow to start. The main reason for this was the Vietnamese administration's lack of familiarity with the various donors' planning and handling procedures and particularly with the international tendering procedures that usually have to be followed in the case of multilateral aid and almost always where Japanese aid is concerned. The capacity of the administration, which has so far effected state investment amounting to about US$ 1 billion p.a. (5 - 7 % of GDP), was initially overextended by an additional volume of several billion US dollars. Consequently, a total of only about US$ 1.8 billion could be absorbed by the end of 1996. From 1997 to 1999 annual disbursements are likely to amount to between US$ 700 and 800 million, equivalent to about 3 % of GDP. With the 8 - 9 % of GDP in the form of private direct investment, this might finance a current account deficit of over 10 % of GDP, albeit with a larger proportion of private funds than the Vietnamese government initially envisaged.

8.3   Structural Adjustment Program with the IMF and World Bank

Although the USA continued to veto financial support for Vietnam from the international financial institutions until 1992, contacts between the Vietnamese government and the IMF and World Bank had begun in the late 1980s. Vietnam saw the clarification of relations with the IMF as essential, since only with its support could there be a settlement of the old debts and thus integration into the international financial system, with the prospect of access to the international financial markets. With a number of technical assistance measures, mostly undertaken through the UNDP, both the IMF and the World Bank began in the late 1980s to forge working contacts with the Vietnamese administration, to train Vietnamese personnel in the core ministries and so to prepare its future financial programs.

The financial support of the international financial institutions became increasingly important for Vietnam after all external sources of funds had been largely blocked from 1990 to 1992 and the restrictive macroeconomic course followed with the utmost consistency in this period did not appear to be permanently sustainable. By this time, moreover, other transforming economies had long since received substantial financial commitments from the IMF and World Bank.

After Vietnam had been able to redeem its outstanding liabilities at the IMF using short-term bridging loans from Japanese and French banks, a first stand-by agreement was reached with the IMF in October 1993 and was followed a year later by a comprehensive agreement with the IMF and World Bank on the implementation of a structural adjustment program. Apart from a Japanese commodity aid loan, the concessionary funds still being provided under this program in 1994 were the first effective financial aid Vietnam received for its reform process.

The conditions attached to the allocation of resources from the IMF's *Enhanced Structural Adjustment Facility (ESAF)* (some US$ 400 million) and the structural adjustment loan from the World Bank's IDA resources (US$ 150 million) conform to the familiar pattern of structural adjustment programs:

–   The IMF and the government agreed on macroeconomic ceilings for domestic credit creation and state borrowing and - a specific feature of the ESAF facility - structural measures in the areas of foreign trade liberalization and the reform of the state-owned enterprises.

–   The World Bank agreed a wide range of reform measures in the state sector aimed at promoting private investment and alleviating poverty, in some cases with very detailed agreements on legal and institutional changes.

A *Policy Framework Paper* on which agreement has been reached between the Vietnamese government and the IMF and World Bank each year for three years at a time since 1995 largely sets the timetable for the reforms. Among the important measures taken in the first two years of the program were a medium-term *Public Investment Program* established under the World Bank's supervision with a view to rationalizing public investment, a *Public Expenditure Review* designed to increase the efficiency of state spending on consumption and a comprehensive audit of the four state-owned commercial banks' balance sheets by international auditing companies. The structural adjustment loans were disbursed on schedule in the first two years of the program. While the macroeconomic conditions were largely observed and the macroeconomic targets were in some cases exceeded, the agreed structural reform suffered numerous delays: "... the rate of implementation has been mixed. However, even in the areas where there have been delays, some progress has been made." (Vietnam - Policy Framework Paper, 1996-98, p. 2).

The international financial institutions have obviously rated persistently high growth and macroeconomic stability higher than the government's hesitant attitude, especially towards the reform of the state sector. This restraint in the assessment of the actual progress made by the reforms is undoubtedly due in part to the belief that little was to be achieved by exerting greater pressure on the government with, say, threats of the suspension of disbursements. The structural adjustment program relies on strong Vietnamese ownership and is not regarded as an IMF/World Bank program in public; there is no mention of conditionality in the debate on economic policy. Nurturing a constructive working atmosphere between the government and the international financial institutions is therefore seen by the IMF and World Bank as more conducive to the reform process than a conflictive strategy.

This restraint in the practical implementation of the reforms is not shared by all donors. Before the fourth meeting of the *Consultative Group* in December 1996, for example, the UNDP presented a highly critical appraisal of the reforms, especially with regard to the heavy investment in capital-intensive state-owned enterprises. The commitment of US$ 2.4 billion by the *Consultative Group* was seen as sending a wrong signal, particularly by representatives of foreign enterprises.[1]

The World Bank, on the other hand, is relying on the long-term leverage of its policy dialogue, which is linked to the program and project loans. With some US$ 500 million each year for five or six projects in the areas of policy reform/structural adjustment (about 25 %), rural poverty/environment (50 %) and infrastructure (25 %) (World Bank 1995d), it will be the most important actor in the policy dialogue in the medium term. The second structural adjustment loan planned for 1997 is to focus on the various problems surrounding land use rights.

In the discussion of the *Policy Framework Paper* for the period 1997-99, however, the IMF, World Bank and Vietnamese government failed to agree on major structural reforms, especially as regards the reduction of the protection of state-owned enterprises. In April 1997 the disbursement of structural adjustment loans was therefore suspended indefinitely.

8.4   Development Cooperation with the Federal Republic of Germany

Vietnam received from the Federal Republic of Germany commitments of official development assistance totaling about DM 120 million from 1990 to 1994 and DM 100 million in both 1995 and 1996. Two thirds of this assistance consisted of grants and loans under the financial co-operation heading, one third of technical cooperation. To this must be added government contributions towards scholarships and training schemes, projects implemented by private organizations - such as the political foundations - and activities undertaken by the Foreign Office (disaster relief) and the *Länder*.

German-Vietnamese development cooperation focuses on:

–   support for the reform policy, including the promotion of the private sector, by means of a broad range of projects in which advice is given on the reform of the economy, the banking system, financial policy, the public administration and the legal system and the development of a public audit office. The private sector is assisted in projects that support small- and medium-scale industry and vocational training;

–   the preservation of natural resources, including agriculture and forestry, by means of reafforestation and rural development projects in various parts of the country;

–   the strengthening of human resources, including education and health, by means of projects designed to assist primary health services, family planning, self-help-oriented poverty alleviation, rural banking and water supply;

- the expansion of the transport system, especially through support for the Vietnamese railways;

- the reintegration of Vietnamese skilled workers employed and trained in the former GDR, through the promotion of newly established firms and vocational integration.

When cooperation began in the early 1990s, a number of projects on which the GDR and Vietnam had agreed were taken over. Some of these projects, in the health sector, for example, were transferred to non-governmental organizations; others, such as the large agricultural projects in coffee and rubber production, continued for a few more years even though their size and orientation towards the state planned economy did not conform to the concept and options of Federal German development cooperation.

Like development cooperation as a whole, German-Vietnamese cooperation was bedeviled by major start-up difficulties, which were further exacerbated by differences of opinion over the return of Vietnamese nationals from Germany. The pluralist approach of German development cooperation - with numerous implementing organizations, NGOs, subcontractors and consultancies - came up against a Vietnamese reception structure which was hardly capable of coordinating this wide range and had first to master the administrative routines involved. The disbursement of project resources was therefore very hesitant at first, resulting, as Vietnam sees it, in something of an imbalance between the considerable planning, examination and preparatory effort that went into the projects and what they have so far 'produced' (Radke 1995). Vietnam also had to come to terms with the fact that most of the benefits it would derive from technical cooperation - which, after all, accounted for about a third of the commitments - would be no more than indirect, through the consultancy and training provided in these projects, which include little in the way of financial transfers.

In some important areas of activity, such as the promotion of small- and medium-scale industry and vocational training, the success of projects suffers from the lack of coherent sectoral policies in Vietnam. Projects often attempt to launch from below processes that are not promoted and are at times even blocked from above. In view of the wide range of projects and implementing organizations in various sectors and the rare attempts to achieve a larger negotiating mass through the program-oriented pooling of projects and the combination of technical and financial cooperation, the options open to German development cooperation to influence conditions appropriately are very limited. Although the UNDP office in Hanoi offers to coordinate the activities of donors at sectoral level, it is an opportunity that has seldom been seized by the bilateral donors.

Responsibility for the appropriate integration of development cooperation projects into sectoral development concepts is thus left to Vietnam, which is having some difficulty in view of the huge backlog of problems in many sectors, the inefficiency of the administration and the internal differences of opinion in some areas of policy.

The impact of development cooperation could probably be increased if mechanisms for a joint sectoral dialogue with the Vietnamese government, which might serve as a guide for the bilateral donors' project activities, were developed by the donors at a level below the *Consultative Group*. This is likely to be left largely to the World Bank, since it alone has the necessary combination of financial negotiating mass and conceptual know-how. It would therefore be all the more important for the bilateral donors to make conceptual contributions to the dialogue between the World Bank and the Vietnamese government in the sectors to which they attach particular importance.

9   The Political Economy of the Transformation Process

A Dilemma: Political Stability or Reform?

Vietnam's transformation from planned to market economy has so far been influenced by the political leadership's determination to see the party continuing to dominate, to prevent political pluralism and multi-party democracy and to resist all foreign efforts in favor of a "peaceful evolution".

Indeed, a decade after the reform process began, the country's political order has hardly changed. Although the 1992 constitution approved greater independence of government and administration from the party and there is now more open discussion - in the preparations for elections, in the press and in the parliament, for example - than there was in the past, the dominant role of the Communist Party and the consequent limits to the emergence of civilian institutions, democratic participation and open social debate have remained largely unchallenged.

What has changed, on the other hand, is the basis for the party's legitimation. Until well into the 1980s it had been determined by the party's role in the national struggle for liberation since the 1940s and the unification of the country that was ultimately achieved. This legitimation of the party, with its distinctly nationalistic bias, which distinguished it from many other communist parties where its popular support was concerned, gradually lost its cohesive force with the obvious failure of the economic policy after unification. This was not the least reason for the growth of willingness to accept reforms in the 1980s, even among conservative cadres. However, they saw the reforms not as a change of system but rather as a tactical concession limited to the economy, with the saving of socialism as the ultimate goal of development. Orthodox and reform forces in the party always agreed that without economic successes the party would lose popular support. The party's role has since been de facto legitimized by a new "social contract": as long as tangible economic progress is made for the people, the party may continue to claim power unchallenged and is indeed seen by large sections of the population - which tends to be impartial in its attitude towards ideological issues - as the lesser evil when compared to a potentially destabilizing multi-party system. This, however, poses a dilemma for the party's policy: the more successful the economic policy, the greater the pressure on the government and party to keep the dynamism in check while rapidly adjusting the institutional structures - often at the expense of their own power. Any slowing of this trend would be bound to erode the party's legitimation as the driving force behind 'industrialization and modernization' and the opening up of Vietnam to international development.

In much of the economy the party has so far been very successful in stimulating reform processes and yet retaining its influence. The commercialization of the state sector in particular has made it possible to promote institutional change and yet to maintain the political control that would have been lost - as the party sees it - if it had permitted privatization. The time will come, however, when, as pointed out in Chapter 5, this strategy will no longer be viable. For one thing, the development of the private sector is being seriously impeded; for another, the roles of the state as entrepreneur and regulator are merging in a way that is already restricting the capacity of the government economic policy to function when access to the market is, for example, limited to the benefit of state actors.

The question of ownership, i.e. the weight carried by and the legal environment for private, cooperative and state property, makes it particularly clear that the party has yet to find a viable solution to the dilemma of orientation towards reforms and holding on to power. The preference given to the promotion of the state sector and the political propaganda for a virtually non-existent cooperative sector will have to be replaced in the medium term with a clear strategy for the promotion of private-sector involvement if the process of catching up is not to lose momentum. From the hesitant policy pursued by the party and government with regard to the rearrangement of the system of ownership it is clear that the transformation process is above all else a process of redistributing property rights - to existing assets and to newly emerging assets. The leading stratum of the old system in the party, government, administrative apparatus and state-owned enterprises was not prepared simply to give up its access to the country's productive resources - outside the agricultural sector at least - as the transformation process went ahead. In view of the internal shortage of capital the direct transfer of much of the state's and society's property to private owners would, moreover, have been bound to give foreign investors - and especially expatriate Vietnamese, who are viewed with suspicion - far too much influence.

Although the interim solution to the ownership problem that was found during the first phase of transformation - largely refraining from privatizing the state-owned enterprises, linking foreign capital to the state sector, blocking the accumulation of capital in private enterprises and protecting autonomous, commercially active parastatal actors - proved successful initially, it is doubtful that this mixture of state capitalism and market socialism will be a suitable basis for a process of industrial modernization, which is still very much in its infancy.

Limited State Control

In the field of tension between stabilization and reform the compromise between conservative and reform forces is usually the crucial basis for changes, the compromise formulae adopted often falling far short of the results sought by the reform forces - and by foreign advisers and investors. The gradualism of reform is therefore nothing other than the expression of conflicts within the leadership over the political direction to be followed and of a lack of consensus on the continuation or the pace of reform.

There was no fixed reform concept, no blueprint for transformation in Vietnam. Every step, starting with the early reform experiments at the beginning of the 1980s, was the outcome of a process of political negotiation within the collective leadership, i.e. without any one person leaving his stamp on the process. Typical of the distribution of forces in this process was that in bad times the upper hand was retained by the reformers, in good times - as evident from the decisions taken at the 8th Party Congress in June 1996, which were felt to have applied the brakes - by the conservative forces. However, as there are many indications that the reform process is making progress even without the state's guiding hand, the government's most important function is to ensure macroeconomic stability. The driving forces behind the reforms are individual provincial governments, particularly in the south of the country, commercial interests in the state sector and, above all, the private sector, whose importance is likely to increase in the medium term even if it is not represented politically by associations. Added to this there is the reform's own momentum in the financial sector, for example, where the modernization of institutions, in conjunction with a critical mass of well trained personnel, is stimulating autonomous modernization processes unseen by political eyes. From the outset these mutually strengthening forces were more important than state control for the continuation of the reforms. Once a number of basic decisions on the direction to be followed had been taken, particularly the decisions on the decollectivization of agriculture, the price reforms and the general freedom given to trade and industry, the reform process assumed a momentum of its own, which can be slowed, but no longer completely halted. Central government reacts rather than controls the course the process is taking.

Against this background the continuation of the reforms is more a matter of muddling through and taking inconsistent decisions than of clear reform designs. Given the lack of internal pressure for reforms, policy is increasingly determined by the pressures associated with the internationalization of the economy: integration into the Asian region, the need for an active locational policy for international investors, the achievement of international creditworthiness and the goal of accession to the WTO or of most-favored-nation status in the US market. The party and government must accept that they can avoid the pressures of international economic cooperation only at the expense of setbacks for the economy and in foreign policy.

Models of Development

The unstated model for many aspects of the reforms is China. It was an obvious choice if only because of the many similarities in the situations of the two countries when their transformation processes were launched. The ideologically difficult step to the socialist market economy was taken in both countries before there was any sign of the collapse of the Soviet and Eastern European planned economies. China is primarily the model for liberalization in agriculture and for the decision not to proceed with the rapid privatization of state-owned enterprises. The picture of the form the socialist market economy will eventually take is, however, as unclear in Vietnam as it is in China. Although the 8th Party Congress in 1996 reaffirmed the dominance of state and cooperative enterprises over the private sector, the state has no control instruments with which it might force real developments into this ideological straitjacket. It is by no means unlikely that the groups who still account for most of social property in Vietnam today - parts of the bureaucracy, the managers of state-owned enterprises and the military - will gradually break away from direct state influence and be absorbed into a growing private sector. Vietnam would then come close to the social development patterns of other Asian countries in which a clearer distinction is made between the state and private sectors, but the dominant social forces - such as the military in Indonesia and Thailand, the state parties in Taiwan and Singapore - play a central role in the private sector and so give the development process a distinctly nationalistic and also corporatist bias.

The leading groups in the party, bureaucracy and business and research communities in Vietnam are undergoing a learning process on which tight limits are formally imposed by decisions taken at the Party Congress, but in which the unprejudiced examination of the experience of other countries, such as Korea and its industrialization policy, Malaysia and its social policy and Indonesia and its poverty alleviation policy, has its place. Much as in China, experimental projects, such as the equitization of a small number of state-owned enterprises, are not difficult to undertake. This receptiveness to pragmatic problem-solving approaches, coupled with the unconditional desire to overcome economic backwardness, makes the transformation process seem more open than the Party Congress decisions indicate.

The examples of the newly industrializing countries in South-East Asia show that there are many variants of successful market-economy systems, and although they are not specifically 'chosen', they are very much guided by the various historical, cultural and economic patterns of development. The features that successful development strategies have in common, the fundamental factors of the Asian economic miracle by which Vietnam too should be guided, are essentially the comparatively high investment in human resources, high propensities to save and invest, macroeconomic stability and the flexible accommodation of the private sector.[1] With a stable macroeconomic situation and an investment ratio that has meanwhile risen to the East Asian level, Vietnam has created a satisfactory starting position for itself in the first decade of transformation. The increased promotion of education and health and a change of policy towards the private sector are the crucial challenges of the next decade of the transformation process.

In view of Vietnam's growing integration into the region, the wide-ranging contacts within the ASEAN framework and global information opportunities, which the government can do little to curb, the internationalization of the economy and society in Vietnam, as in the other South-East Asian countries, can no longer be prevented. It would be fatal if Vietnam failed to seize the consequent opportunities and again went its own way after the long and costly detours in its history.

Notes

Chapter 1

1   See World Bank (1993). Asked what was the greatest opportunity missed in recent decades, the former Vietnamese Foreign Minister Nguyen Co Thach replied: *"Missing the chance to develop Vietnam, at a time when the world made its greatest economic strides in history."* Far Eastern Economic Review, 21 March 1996, p. 38.

2   As a limited number of these focal areas has had to be chosen, it cannot be claimed that a comprehensive analysis of the Vietnamese transformation process is made here. Such an analysis would also have to cover, for example, the problems associated with agricultural development and the reform of the legal system and public administration.

Chapter 2

1   After a process of growing alienation from China, Vietnam had joined the CMEA in 1978. The CMEA member countries increased the economic aid they gave to Vietnam in the form of commodities and capital projects, especially in primary industries. In return, Vietnam exported raw materials and light industrial goods, but it was never fully integrated into the CMEA's specific division of labor.

2   This was primarily necessary in the case of foodstuffs, since only a rise in government purchase prices encouraged the peasants to increase supplies to the state.

3   Private financial assets were hardly affected by the currency reform because they were held in gold and foreign exchange; Vo Nhan Tri (1990), p. 143.

4   Simpler forms of collective cooperation in agriculture - such as the joint introduction and maintenance of irrigation systems - had been accepted by the peasants when collectivization began. It was only the actual confiscation of property, and especially of draft animals, and the employment of the peasants on activities from which they derived no benefit that were resisted. As the plots farmed are mostly very small, purchasing, marketing or credit cooperatives or cooperatives to look after common property can play a very useful role.

5   A total of more than 2 million Vietnamese live abroad. Of particular relevance to the south of the country in this context are the collaborators of the South Vietnamese regime who emigrated in 1975/76 and the traders and industrialists exiled in 1977/78, many of whom have prospered, particularly in the USA. Of

less economic significance are the boat people who have emigrated to many different countries since 1979 and the Vietnamese who emigrated mostly from Central and North Vietnam to Eastern Europe and Germany to work, no more than temporarily in most cases.

6   Dapice / Perkins / Haughton (1996), Chapter I, p. 7. The agricultural and industrial cooperatives are considered part of the non-state sector even though they were included in the mechanisms of central planning before 1989.

Chapter 3

1   Doanh / McCarty (1995) point out that in more advanced socialist countries the system of repressed inflation worked far better. The retail price index in the Soviet Union, for example, hardly rose from 1960 to 1980 and by 1 % p.a. from 1980 to 1990.

2   "The bureaucratically centralized management mechanism based on state subsidies, which has been in force for many years now, far from creating a driving force for development, has weakened the socialist economy, limited the use and transformation of the other economic sectors, put a brake on production, lowered labor productivity, product quality and economic efficiency, put distribution and circulation in a state of chaos and given rise to numerous negative manifestations in our society." Sixth Party Congress of the Communist Party of Vietnam (15-18 December 1986), quoted from Lipworth / Spittäler (1993), p. 3.

3   The successes of the economic reform in China and the dynamism of the NICs in Asia did not leave the Vietnamese leadership unimpressed. A reduction in Soviet economic aid also had to be expected. It was thus announced at the CMEA Council meeting in 1987 that the deficits of the CMEA developing countries would no longer be financed on the same scale as in the past; Diehl (1993), p. 25.

4   The demand for money caused by the unique effect of a major 'monetization' of the Vietnamese economy absorbed some of the rising money supply created by the considerable domestic credit expansion and so reduced its inflationary effect. Dollar (1993), p. 215.

5   Indirect subsidization in the form of low-interest loans, access to land, foreign trade licenses, etc. continues (see section 5.1).

6   To this end, laws were passed on turnover tax, taxes on profits and excise duties for the non-state sector in 1990 and for the state sector in 1991. Other new taxes are the natural resource tax (oil levy), personal income tax, capital tax and the capital utilization levy (for state-owned enterprises). The Finance

Ministry was reorganized to enable it to perform its new function as the supreme fiscal authority; Lipworth / Spittäler (1993), p. 13.

7   In 1994 the tax ratio (tax revenue as a proportion of GDP) in Thailand was 17 % and in Indonesia 16.3 %; World Bank (1996), p. 214.

8   A debt rescheduling agreement with Russia, the main creditor, has so far been thwarted by differences of opinion over the transfer rouble/US$ exchange rate.

9   For direct investment see section 5.3, for development aid Chapter 8.

Chapter 4

1   The ICOR is the reciprocal value of the output-capital ratio. A lower value signifies high productivity of the capital invested.

2   In South Korea the ICOR in the 1960s and 1970s was 2.5 and later 4. In Indonesia it is 5; thus, at a investment ratio of 30 %, only 6 % growth is generated.

3   The low capital-output ratio from 1992 to 1995 was due to the completion of the large Hoa Binh hydroelectric power station in 1991 and the beginning of oil production in the Bac Ho field, two major investments initially followed by a decline in government capital spending. Heavy infrastructure investment with long maturity periods in the second half of the 1990s will probably lead to a rise in the capital-output ratio.

4   See, e.g., Cho / Khatkhate (1989) for reforms of financial systems in Asia.

5   World Bank (1994), p. 19. These figures are estimates, there being at present no system of classifying credits or appropriate valuation adjustment regulations.

6   The average in the ASEAN countries is about 10 % and less than 20 % in most transforming economies; World Bank (1994), p. 12.

7   "A separate, confidential central bank report puts the level of overdue loans at 54 *joint stock banks* at 13 per cent of their portfolios." Financial Times, 21 August 1996, p. 5 ("Doubts raised over health of Vietnamese banking").

8   "After years of keeping dollars under the mattress, Vietnamese are learning to trust financial institutions again." Financial Times, 30/31 December 1995, p. 3.

Chapter 5

1   The requirements for re-registration included assets of at least US$ 200,000 and the ability to service debts. Many small enterprises were unable to meet these requirements. Their assets (usually consisting solely of buildings and land use rights) were sold and used to repay debts. The criteria were not strictly applied to larger enterprises. In many cases large state-owned enterprises were urged to take over small enterprises so that they might remain in operation. Probert / Young (1995), p. 513.

2   1992 figures, World Bank (1995a), p. 102.

3   The information is obtained from the unpublished *Policy Framework Paper* drawn up by the Vietnamese government jointly with the IMF and World Bank (see Chapter 8).

4   Vietnam Investment Review, 20-26 May 1996, p. 1: "Government to review the private sector."

5   While South Korean, Taiwanese and Japanese investors are primarily involved in manufacturing industry, investment from Hong Kong and Singapore is focused on the real estate sector.

6   At the end of 1995 the State Committee was merged with the State Planning Commission to become the Ministry of Planning and Investment, which is now responsible for the whole authorization procedure.

7   See, for example, Far Eastern Review, 13 July 1995, pp. 60 ff. ("The honeymoon is over"). The Investment Law as amended for the third time in late 1996 requires unanimity only in the case of decisions of principle; in day-to-day business a two-thirds majority is needed.

8   "... the hype that once surrounded Vietnam - some call it Asia's next 'tiger' economy - has given way to a resigned weariness and an understanding that Vietnam, while full of potential, offers few solid opportunities." Far Eastern Economic Review, 28 March 1996, p. 50 ("Vietnam Syndrome").

9   Financial Times, 3 July 1996, p. 4: "Investors in Vietnam face stricter regime".

10   Financial Times, 4 October 1996, p. 4: "Waiting games for Vietnam car makers".

11   The transfer of technology from the public to the semi-private sector played a central role in the success of the Chinese *township and village enterprises*. See, for example, Wong / Ma / Yang (1995).

Chapter 6

1   "... the government does not have trained personnel to evaluate *environmental impact assessments* nor a timeline for compliance or decisions on how to respond to them. The *environmental protection law* has provisions for levying fines against polluters but does not explain how fines will be determined nor who will enforce them, and it prohibits the importation of technology and equipment not meeting environmental standards, but provides no means to monitor equipment imports." Sikor / O'Rourke (1996), p. 607.

Chapter 7

1   The *Vietnam Living Standards Survey* was conducted by the Vietnamese Statistical Office in cooperation with the World Bank; see World Bank (1995c).

Chapter 8

1   Far Eastern Economic Review, 19 December 1996, pp. 70 f. ("Mixed Signals. Hanoi's Reforms called too slow for comfort").

Chapter 9

1   "Each decade had its challenges, and each decade produced government policy responses that turned out, in Kuznet's terms, to have been accommodating rather than obstructive of changes required by mainly private agents." Ranis (1995), p. 510.

Bibliography

Beresford, M. (1989): *National Unification and Economic Development in Vietnam*, London

– (1995): "Interpretation of the Vietnamese Economic Reforms 1979-85" (mimeo)

Bird, R.M. / J.I. Litvack / M. Govinda Rao (1995): "Intergovernmental Fiscal Relations and Poverty Alleviation in Vietnam", World Bank Research Working Paper, Washington

Cho, J. / D. Khatkhate (1989): "Lessons of Financial Liberalization in Asia. A Comparative Study", World Bank Discussion Paper No. 50, Washington

Dang Duc Dam (1995): *Vietnam's Economy 1986-95*, Hanoi

Dapice, D. / D. Perkins / J. Haughton (eds) (1996): *In Search of the Dragon's Tail. Economic Reform in Vietnam*, Harvard Institute for International Development, Cambridge/Mass.

De Vylder, S. / A. Fforde (1988): *Vietnam. An Economy in Transition*, SIDA, Stockholm

Diehl, M. (1993): *Systemtransformation in Vietnam. Liberalisierungserfolge - Stabilisierungsprobleme*, Institut für Weltwirtschaft, Kiel

– (1994): *Real Adjustment in the Economic Transformation Process. The Industrial Sector of Vietnam 1986-92*, Kiel Institute of World Economics, Kiel

– (1995): *Enterprise Adjustment in the Economic Transformation Process. Microeconomic Evidence from Industrial State Enterprises in Northern Vietnam*, Kiel Institute of World Economics, Kiel

Diez, J.R. (1995): "Systemtransformation in Vietnam. Industrieller Strukturwandel und Regionalwirtschaftliche Auswirkungen", in: *Hannoversche Geographische Arbeiten*, Vol. 51, Hannover

Dollar, D. (1995): "Vietnam - Successes and Failures of Macroeconomic Stabilization", in: B. Ljunggren, "Macroeconomic Adjustment and Structural Reform in an Open Transition Economy. The Case of Vietnam", Stockholm (mimeo)

Fforde, A. / A. Goldstone (1995): *Vietnam to 2005 - Advancing on all fronts*, The Economist Intelligence Unit, London

Fforde, A. (1993): "The Political Economy of 'Reform' in Vietnam - Some Reflections", in: B. Ljunggren (ed.), *The Challenge of Reform in Indochina*, Harvard Institute for International Development, Cambridge/Mass.

Gates, C.L. (1995a): "Vietnam's Economic 'Third Way'", in: *Business Times*, 24/25 June, Singapore

– (1995b): "Enterprise Reform and Vietnam's Transformation to a Market-Oriented Economy, in: *ASEAN Economic Bulletin*, July 1995, Manila

IMF (1994): *Economic Review - Vietnam*, Washington

– (1996): *Vietnam - Transition to a Market Economy*, Washington

Jamison, A. / E. Baark (1995): "From Market Reforms to Sustainable Development", in: I. Norlund / C. Gates / V.C. Dam (eds), *Vietnam in a Changing World*, Nordic Institute of Asian Studies, Richmond/Surrey, pp. 277 f.

Kurths, K. (1987): *Private Kleinbetriebe in Vietnam. Rahmenbedingungen und Hemmnisse ihrer Entwicklung*, Saarbrücken, Fort Lauderdale

Le Dang Doanh / A. McCarty (1995): "Economic Reform in Vietnam. Achievements and Prospects", in: S.F. Noya / J.L.H. Tan (eds), *Asian Transitional Economies. Challenges and Prospects for Reform and Transformation*, Institute of Southeast Asian Studies, Singapore

Leipziger, D.M. (1992): *Awakening the Market. Viet Nam's Economic Transition*, World Bank Discussion Paper 157, Washington

Lipworth, G. / E. Spittäler (1993): "Vietnam - Reform and Stabilization. 1986-92", IMF Working Paper, Washington

Ljunggren, B. (1995): "Macroeconomic Adjustment and Structural Reform in an Open Transition Economy. The Case of Vietnam", Stockholm (mimeo)

Meier, R. / N. Pilgrim (1995): *Framework Conditions for Small Enterprise Development in Vietnam*, ZDH-Technonet Asia Partnership Project, Göttingen, Bonn

Probert, J. / D. Young (1995): "The Vietnamese Road to Capitalism. Decentralization, De-facto Privatization and the Limits to Piecemeal Reform", in: *Communist Economies and Economic Transformation*, Vol. 7, No. 4

Radke, D. / P. Wolff (1990): *Ansatzpunkte für die Entwicklungszusammenarbeit zwischen der Bundesrepublik Deutschland und Vietnam*, German Development Institute, Berlin

Radke D., et al. (1992): *Finanzsektorstudie Vietnam. Empfehlungen zum Aufbau eines zweistufigen Finanzsystems*, German Development Institute, Berlin

Radke, D. (1995): "Deutsch-Vietnamesische Kooperationsbeziehungen - die ungenutzten Chancen", in: *Asien*, Vol. 55, Berlin

Ranis, G. (1995): "Another Look at the East Asian Miracle", in: *The World Bank Economic Review*, Vol. 9, No. 3

Reed, D. (ed.) (1996): *Structural Adjustment, the Environment, and Sustainable Development*, World Wide Fund for Nature, London

Scown, M.J. (1995): "Laying Down the Law", in: *Far Eastern Economic Review*, 5 October

Sikor, T.O. / D. O'Rourke (1996): "Economic and Environmental Dynamics of Reform in Vietnam", in: *Asian Survey*, Vol. 36, No. 6

UNDP (1995): "Improving Economic Opportunities for the Rural Poor", Hanoi (mimeo)

Vo Nhan Tri (1990): *Vietnam's Economic Policy since 1975. A Critical Analysis*, Institute of Southeast Asian Studies, Singapore

Wade, R. (1990): *Governing the Market. Economic Theory and the Role of Government in East Asian Industrialization*, Princeton

World Bank (1992): "Development and the Environment", World Development Report 1992, Washington

– (1993): *The East Asian Miracle. Economic Growth and Public Policy*, Washington

– (1994): *Vietnam - Public Sector Management and Private Sector Incentives*, Washington

– (1995a): *Vietnam - Economic Report on Industrialization and Industrial Policy*, Washington

– (1995b): *Vietnam - Environmental Program and Policy Priorities for a Socialist Economy in Transition*, Washington

– (1995c): *Vietnam - Poverty Assessment and Strategy*, Washington

– (1995d): *Vietnam - Country Assistance Strategy*, Washington

– (1996): "From Plan to Market", World Development Report 1996, Washington

Wolff, P., et al. (1995): *Finanzierung von kleinen und mittleren Unternehmen in Vietnam*, German Development Institute, Berlin

Wong, J. / Rong Ma / Mu Yang (eds) (1995): *China's Rural Enterprises. Ten Case Studies*, Singapore

Zhang, Z. (1996): "AFTA and APEC, with Policy Implications for Vietnam's Trade and FDI", in: *Development Policy Review*, Vol. 14, No. 3